T0063057

Fig. 1 Victoria City Hall: Poets were proud of the developing city as exemplified by its expanded City Hall (finished in 1890; designed by John Teague) and its electric streetcar system (the first in Canada), but some were critical of the municipal government and others had doubts about the efficiency of the new trams. *(Williams' Official British Columbia Directory,* Part 1, 1892)

IMPERIAL EDEN

VICTORIA BC IN VERSE
c. 1858-1920

Robert Ratcliffe Taylor

Order this book online at www.trafford.com
or email orders@trafford.com

Most Trafford titles are also available at major online book retailers.

Printed in the United States of America.

ISBN: 978-1-4907-5003-3 (sc)
ISBN: 978-1-4907-5010-1 (hc)
ISBN: 978-1-4907-5004-0 (e)

Library of Congress Control Number: 2014919293

Trafford rev. 11/10/2014

www.trafford.com

North America & international
toll-free: 1 888 232 4444 (USA & Canada)
fax: 812 355 4082

NOTE: Short portions of this book have appeared in the following of my publications:

"The Mark of the Hun. The Image of Germans in Popular Verse Published in Victoria, B.C., during the Great War," *British Columbia History.* Vol. 42, No. 3, 2-7.

The Ones Who Have to Pay. The Soldier-Poets of Victoria B.C. in the Great War 1914-18. Bloomington, IN: Trafford, 2013.

"A Note on Some 'Lost' Poems by Robert W. Service", *Canadian Poetry/Studies/Documents/Reviews.* No. 62, Spring/Summer, 2008, 80-86.

CONTENTS

LIST OF ILLUSTRATIONS

ACKNOWLEDGEMENTS

Research for this book was made easier by the friendly assistance of the staff at the Archives of British Columbia, the Victoria City Archives, the Local History Room at the Victoria Public Library and the Microforms Room at the University of Victoria.

I owe a debt of gratitude to Kevin McCabe of Blarneystone Publications for first suggesting a book with this theme. I am especially indebted to Dr. D. Gillian Thompson for her constructive criticism and encouragement. As usual, my wife Anne offered constant support. Of course, any misconceptions or errors in this book are my own responsibility.

BEFOREHAND

In the late nineteenth century, many poets lauded British Columbia's capital as both an idyllic paradise and an outpost of the British Empire. Ironically, Victorians' love of the Empire and its military glory led them enthusiastically into the Great War of 1914-1918, a conflict which helped to end both their relatively paradisal isolation and their love of things British. Such is the theme of this essay.

Readers who are not interested in the historical background of the poems can skip the first section. Other readers may want simply to dip into the poetry here and there, as the section titles interest them.

TO BEGIN

In his history of late nineteenth century Victoria, local writer Derek Pethick records the pride, confidence and optimism of local people who believed they were living on a "blessed isle".* Indeed, many pre-1914 Victorians often expressed a sense of delight in both their geographical setting and their ethnic heritage, as their poems published in local newspapers and magazines reveal.

Reading these old periodicals is both challenging and rewarding. Even if you don't understand the intricacies of political history a century ago, the caricatures can be amusing. In the twenty-first century, of course, some of the jokes and the "funny papers" can still provoke chuckles. The commercial advertisements reveal people's concerns and worries back then — even if the products sometimes seem absurd. Especially interesting are the poems which were regularly printed in Victoria's several newspapers and journals in the period c. 1858-1920. Their subjects were many. Poets often admired local scenery or important persons. Some wrote political satire; others, advertisements for products on sale. A few are obscure in their references, while others can astonish us by their relevance to twenty-first century Victoria.

Local citizens writing to the editors often wrote in verse. The purpose of this book is to show that many of the poems are records of the values and concerns of our great-grandparents a hundred years ago.

---

* *Summer of Promise. Victoria 1864-1914*, Victoria: Sono Nis, 1980, 187.

THE SITUATION AT ESQUIMALT.

(Depicted by Miss Emily Carr.)

Fig. 2 A Mutual Sorrow: When the Imperial navy abandoned Esquimalt, some locals, such as the artist Emily Carr (1871-1945) may have felt abandoned by Great Britain but she, like many Victorians, expressed herself in prose and verse (as well as in paint). (*The Week,* 25 February 1905)

The poems here were submitted to and were published by the editors of Victoria newspapers and journals. Occasionally they printed works written by poets who never saw Victoria and were not thinking of the city when they wrote, but whose verse was deemed relevant to Victoria by editors. (I have also occasionally included a few works published in edited compilations.) In the process of my research, I have sometimes made discoveries which are amusing and revealing, as in a poem by the artist Emily Carr (1871-1945) which, accompanied by her illustration, was published on page one of Victoria's *The Week*, on 25 February 1905:

There's a silver Sockeye Salmon
Swimming round Esquimalt Bay
And his tail is curled in anguish
Tears are in his eyes they say
There's a melancholy Middie[*]
Uniformed in blue and gold,
Woeful wailing by the water —
Very downcast, I am told.
Why oh Salmon? Why oh Middie?
Mourn you, sigh you, fret and weep,
Is some shadow o'er Esquimalt
Brooding o'er its waters deep?
Aye 'tis sounds of coming, going,
Sad farewells for fish and man,
For the middie different waters
For the fish:— a can.

Here Carr— and presumably other locals (but perhaps not fish) — lamented the termination of Britain's Pacific Command on 1 March 1905, when Canada assumed responsibility for its own naval defence. We knew that Carr was an accomplished prose writer (not

---

* A "middie" was a midshipman.

to mention a superlative painter!), but apparently she also tried her hand at political cartooning — and verse. As well, several poems by the "Bard of the Yukon", Robert Service (1874-1958), written while he was employed as a bank clerk here, appeared in the *Victoria Daily Colonist*. Similar surprises, as well as humour and insights into Victoria life over a century ago, are found in the following pages.

I have given the complete text of most of the poems reproduced here. Occasionally, however, the verbosity of the poet has necessitated the omission of some lines — indicated by an ellipsis ("... ").

Of course, this book cannot present a complete picture of Victorians' beliefs and opinions. Some might argue that such poetry was an expressive only of the literate, articulate, political and social elite who created the tone of the culture. And they would be partly correct. But in fact some of the "lower orders" wrote verse and are represented in these pages — which testifies to the popularity of poetry-writing and the ubiquitousness of certain "mentalities" at the time.

Nevertheless, my readers may want to know why I have dedicated a whole book to poetry published in Victoria so long ago.

PART ONE

Victoria in Verse

WHY VERSE?

When many twenty-first century people hear the word "poetry", their eyes glaze over and their brains freeze. And why not? Much "modern" verse is highly intellectual and deeply abstruse. Moreover, many of us recall dreary "English Lit" classes in high school taught by teachers who never felt the sensual rush provided by a truly fine poem. Yet, in the 19th century, many Victoria writers, editors and readers loved poetry and, by extension, the English language itself — and its idiosyncrasies. In 1860, for example, the *Victoria British Colonist* delighted in "An English Orthograph Puzzle", by an anonymous poet:

Wife, make me some dumplings of dough,
They're better than meat for my cough;
Pray let them be boiled 'til hot through,
But not 'til they're heavy or tough.

Now I must be off to the plough,
And the boys (when they've had enough)
Must keep the flies off with a bough,
While the old mare drinks at the trough.

(*The British Colonist,* 3 January 1860)

Other poets reveled in creating vivid word-pictures. On the front page of its weekend supplement for 29 March 1908, for example, the

Victoria *Daily Colonist* printed a poem by the English immigrant and sportsman Clive **Phillips-Wolley** (1854 - 1918):

The Salmon Run

Vague space, and in the hush Dawn's pencil drew
On the damp clouds of darkness, line by line,
Peaks and vast headlands, and a fresh wind blew
Sharp with the stinging kisses of the brine,
Pungent with perfume of the sunburnt pine.

Through drifting veils of filmy forest smoke,
Filtered the rose-pink sunrise of the day.
The sea plains heaved; the tide-rip laughing woke;
Beyond the sun-limned circle of the bay
Ocean, a palpitating opal, lay,

Milk-white mysterious. Throbbing faery fire
Coursed through its veins and all the madcap throng
Which cradles in the tide-rip, oceans choir,
In stoles of roughened silver, deep-voiced, strong,
Danced as it sang the young tide's meeting song,

Working the sea to madness. Sudden waves
Roared by the cliffs, fretted the canopies
Written with runes, and echoed in the caves.
There was no wind to swing the slender trees
And yet through fields of calm ran racing seas.

Strange eddies came and went. The blacktoothed rocks
Were whelmed in waters piled upon an heap [sic].
Louder and louder grew the thunder-shocks
Of the tempestous rip. Beyond, the Deep
Lay calm and smiling, mother-like, asleep.

Then fell a miracle. The waters knew
Some deep sea-call, and their swift tides became
Incarnate, and sudden incarnate grew
Their shifting light. Argent and azure flame
Drave through the Deep. The salmon pilgrims came.

A foredoomed pilgrimage from depths profound
To grey Alaskan waters, turgid, pent
In mildewed pines, where neither sun nor sound
Of oceans' song can reach — the last event
To rot on glacial mud, frayed, leprous, spent.

Not every poem published by Victoria's newspapers a century ago was so extravagant in its imagery. Some were painfully precise. When "A Local Poet" viewed the "James Bay Mud Flats" in the Victoria *Daily Colonist* for 17 June 1904, he wrote simply,

When I survey the wondrous flats
I always stop and think,
And put my fingers to my nose
To guard away the stink.

But very soon it will be gone,
No more offensive smell,
And what will be the city's pride
The C.P.R. Hotel.

The hotel would be the Empress, opened in 1908. (See also the "Suspect's" poem below.)

This book is full of poems, both effulgent or concise. None of them, of course, will ever appear in the *Oxford Book of English Verse.* The fact that someone felt strongly enough to write them, however, and someone else believed that their poems were important enough to publish gives them significance as a kind of historical evidence. Some would argue that they convey feelings and ideas more intensely and more clearly than do prose works.

Before we consider why such verse is useful to students of Victoria's past, we should ask: what exactly is a poem? Poetry is a response in words to a vivid experience or an encounter with a striking idea or emotion. When I exclaim, "What a beautiful sunset!", I'm speaking poetically because I have identified a vivid experience and described it in a subjective way. However, my lovely sunset may be your cloudy horizon at dusk! There's a subjective element in our definition of a poem. More is required and it seems that a poem must be expressed in language that is memorable and structured in some way. The poet, whether a teenaged lover or a mature poet laureate, puts his or her profound experience into measured and ordered form in the hope of making sense of it and preserving it. (The equivalent, for most of us ungifted people, is taking photographs of a family vacation, wedding, or graduation.)

Poetry can appear in Shakespearean blank verse, in 20th century free verse, in rhyming couplets, in seventeen syllables (as in Japanese haiku), in limericks, etc. etc. etc. Prose itself can often sound like poetry. In fact, there may be as many forms of poetry as there are poems in any language! What is important about the structure of a poem is that it makes the poem more striking to the reader or listener and may also aid in remembering it. The kind of verse found in this book usually employs metre and rhyme, which made it easy for our great-grandparents to remember, memorize or even recite it.

Instinctively, we are drawn to rhyme and rhythm — as children, and as adults, too. We remember songs, not only because of their tunes but because of their words, which may be alliterative or rhyming. Even the most un-literary of us may have in the back of our mind the words of a raunchy limerick or two. As children, we naturally make up or recite rhymes to skip by or to taunt others with. As high school students, we may have been lucky enough — although we may not have thought so at the time —to have been compelled to memorize a passage from Shakespeare or an ode by John Keats. As college students, some of us even tried to express our late adolescent *Sturm und Drang* in midnight-scribbled verse. This seemed natural at the time, although we may have destroyed our efforts long ago.

When Theodor Adorno wrote that, "To still write a poem after Auschwitz is barbaric", his despair was all too understandable. But he may have been excessively pessimistic, because the popularity of poetry waxes and wanes. In some eras it is all around us. In others, no one reads it (although people may still write it, if only privately, not for publication or recitation). In the early 21st century, poetry seems to have enjoyed a feeble renaissance, with, for example, the creation of the position of a Canadian national "poet laureate". Certain groups, such as the Canadian Authors Association, keep poetry alive in annual anthologies or chapbooks. The Ontario Poetry Society and Poets Podium, for example, have encouraged the writing and publishing of members' poetry — in blank verse, free verse, rhyme — even in forms such as the sonnet or villanelle. We can read poetry on the walls of busses and subway cars. Academic and literary journals, such as *Fiddlehead* or *The Malahat Review*, serve more abstruse interests. On the other hand, just as the ability (or desire) to write melody seems extinct in both our classical and popular composers, so too the interest in rhyme and rhythm seems defunct today. Some scholars refer to "a great divide" which developed after World War One when romanticism in literature declined, followed by rational intellectualizing, especially in poetry.

Consequently, what is considered "good" poetry today is often unintelligible even to the sensitive, educated person.

Often it's too personal or intellectual to make sense to readers or listeners, other than to a select coterie. Such "post-modern" or "deconstructionist" works rarely make it into popular journals or magazines. In fact, poetry of any kind rarely appears today in local newspapers, even in weekend supplements.

It was not always so. In the 19th and early 20th centuries, poems were published on the front pages of newspapers, such as Victoria's *Daily Colonist* or the *Victoria Daily Times*. Of course, such dailies, like their counterparts in other communities which served a particular city and its hinterland — in this case Victoria and southern Vancouver Island — printed news about that area and reflected the interests of its citizens as well as poetry. It was significant, however, that the ability to conjure up a verse for a social occasion was considered a normal accomplishment civilized ladies or gentlemen, who did not hesitate to offer their verses for publication and were sometimes successful. In fact, Victoria newspapers even published poems which were identified as the works of children.

Some poems were by well-known local poets; others, by writers famous in the English-speaking world. But some occasionally came from what may seem to be unexpected sources. For example, **James L. Dunn** (d. 1890), captain of the HBC clipper ship TITANIA, was known as a "popular and good-hearted master" (*Colonist*, 17 October 1890, 5). When his ship was moored in Esquimalt on 22 September 1889, he wrote,

Farewell to Victoria, 1889

Kind friends in Victoria, the time is now nigh
When, sailing for England, I must bid you good bye;
But shall carry this feeling, you must not think me vain,
Next year you'll be pleased to see me again.

The beautiful clipper that I'm proud to command
Four times has returned to this much favored land;
The "Titania" is now a true household word,
For she's tight, staunch and strong, and fleet as a bird.

Yet oft I'll remember the bright, happy hours
I have spent in your homes all embosomed with flowers;
For this is your rule, and it is no vain boast,
"To welcome the stranger who visits your coast."

In grandeur sublime, majestic and high,
Mount Baker uplifts its proud peak to the sky;
Whilst the mounts of Olympus, from Heaven's blue
dome,
Keep watch o'er the Straits that front your sweet home.

Victoria, fair city! I predict that kind fate
Your childhood will change to a prime that is great;
Here's success to all those that in you now dwell,
Accept my best wishes, God speed you, farewell.

Two days later, the *Colonist* saw fit to publish these verses on its editorial page. The TITANIA was a Hudson's Bay Company cargo clipper, engaged in the Far Eastern tea trade. Obviously, Victoria and its environs had made a positive impression on the captain, especially the beautiful geographical setting of the city, which many were already describing as "paradise". He had probably also spent some happy social hours among the city's commercial and business elite. The poem reminds us that in the nineteenth century, ships and seafarers (long before cruise liners and tourists) played a vital role in the economic and social life of the city. Moreover, the captain himself — probably a down-to–earth practical seafarer — felt no embarrassment in putting his feelings into verse for publication. He is a good example of the sort of person who tried to put powerful sensations into structured, metered, and rhyming form and wanted to share them with readers. His poem is not great art, but it gives us a sense of social and literary life in Victoria over a century ago.

Fig. 3 Titles of Poetry Columns in the Daily Colonist: The *Colonist* enthusiastically promoted local poets but occasionally mocked its own seriousness. Poems in these columns were probably written by the editors and usually commented on political events and social mores. (*Victoria Daily Colonist*, 2 and 16 April 1911)

The 23rd of December 1918 saw a brief entry in the *Times* of that day, punning on the use of gas for lighting and cooking in Victoria households:

The Editor — My dear sir, we can't publish nonsense like this —
it's not poetry at all. It's an escape of gas."
Poet — "Ah, I see. Something wrong with the meter".

If this joke seems forced, nevertheless editors, poets and readers alike were concerned with what they thought was good verse. In many of these poems, therefore, the language is often Biblical in inspiration ("thee", "thou", etc.) or Shakespearean (contractions such as "o'er" and "'neath"). Of course, c. 1900 Victoria people did not speak this way but writers believed that use of this archaic language gave weight to their expression. As well, they had been taught in school the importance of rhyme schemes, metre (the rhythmic structure of a poem), and feet (stressed or unstressed syllables).

Even in amateur literary circles at that time, strict rules prevailed as to what was acceptable in verse. On 23 December 1918, the Victoria *Daily Times*, published a poem by one "**GLESK**", who would identify himself only as a member of the Great War Veterans' Association. He had been offended by some verses which had earlier appeared in the *Times* and fired off this salvo:

O "Dawn", who wrote that little verse
I read in Thursday's Times,
'Twas to the point, pithy and terse,
But — who could say it rhymes?
For one with a musician's ear

'Tis nothing short of pain
To make "meet" rhyme with "peace". Your gear
Was out of work what time, I fear,
You wrote your sweet refrain.

Poetic license might endorse
Your rhyming "board" with "word",
But never "thought" with "not". Of course,
It may not have occurred
To you that "us" and "wireless"
Rhyme not, although your scan
Is pretty good, but what a mess
You made of rhyme, O Man!

Of course, editors chose which poems (whether in traditional or unusual form) to print. Much earlier (7 May 1859), the *Victoria Weekly Gazette* had noted, "There are two kinds of poetry which it is very difficult to refuse to publish. One is exceedingly good, the other execrably bad . . .". Admittedly, by any standards, some of the published poetry was not very good. Yet some awkward rhymes were deliberately funny. In 1892, the *Colonist* noted wryly that "Mr. W.H. Snider of Spring Ridge, received a large pumpkin yesterday as a present from his friend and neighbour, Barrister S. Perry Mills. The pumpkin was grown by Mr. M. at his residence on Fernwood Road . . . 4 feet 6 inches in circumference and weighed nearly . . . 100 pounds," which moved the poetry editor to write,

The Lay of the Last Pumpkin

Mr. Mills, he had a pumpkin
And it grew and it grew,
And it grew upon a vine.
Its size was six by nine,
And he said "It is mine",
And it grew.

"Oh what with my big pumpkin
Shall I do? Shall I do?"
And so stood beside her,
Often tried he to decide her.
Then said to Mr. Snider,
"It's for you".

(*Colonist*, 6 November 1892)
The poet probably knew how awkward his "verse" was — and that was just the joke. Was this a parody of free verse (which tried to follow the natural speech rhythm) and which was becoming popular with some writers at the time? At all events, giant pumpkins still command space in the *Times/Colonist* and other newspapers, although not usually accompanied by poetry, rhyming or not.

In the early twentieth century, one form of verse was especially popular: the limerick. Local journals used this type of poetry in contests, presumably to increase their circulation. On one occasion, the *Times* celebrated the opening of the annual fall fair at the Willows with such a contest, asking their readers to complete the following:

Be sure you attend the Fall Fair.
For the women's new building is there,
Art, music, you'll find,
Food for body and mind.
(Fifth line should be rhyming with fair).

(*Times*, 13 October 1909) On this occasion, to the consternation of entrants, the box containing the entries went missing. The periodical, *The Week,* on 11 November 1911, also announced a limerick contest. Entrants had to complete the following:

If you wish to be happy and wise
You must first win a Limerick prize.
For dollars are things
That seem to have wings,
. . . .

Contestants had to submit fifty cents with each completed limerick. The prize was a monetary one, but a portion of the total sum collected would be donated to the Public Library for book purchases; in a contest of December 1911, that portion would be given to the Jubilee Hospital.

Given the use of pseudonyms, initials, and "anonymous", I have sometimes found it impossible to identify some writers. But occasionally the editor will note that the writer was a Victoria resident. Then, using censuses and directories, I have often been able to learn biographical details about certain local poets and have inserted the data here. Very possibly some "anonymous" poets or those identified only by initials were the editors of the publications.

For example, the editor of the *Victoria Home Journal* confessed on 25 February 1893, "I occasionally lapse into a poetic vein". He may have used the pseudonyms "Guff" or "Pere Grinator" which were appended to some verses in the *Journal.*

The preceding examples of verse should give the impression that poetry was very popular in Victoria a century ago, as indeed it was, but . . .

WHY VICTORIA?

In certain ways, Victoria was — and is — an unusual city, partly because of its geographical location (which has inspired generations of poets and artists) and partly because of its inhabitants' relatively high degree of literacy and appreciation of the arts. Compared to other pioneer communities in Western Canada, Victoria was sophisticated. Very quickly the rugged fur trading outpost, founded in 1843, began to look different from other contemporary settlements because, on its farms and estates, the owners tried to recreate a lifestyle which they had known in Britain. Even within Fort Victoria, the standard of living was relatively high, with the mess room being set with linen tablecloths and crystal decanters, flanked by Windsor chairs. If London's plan to stock the colony with men of upper class birth and education was never fully worked out, nevertheless a high level of what contemporaries called "refinement" and "culture" prevailed.

On the other hand, insofar as later nineteenth century Victoria residents enjoyed poetry, they were not unusual. Across Canada, verse had never been and never would be again as popular. For many of our great-grandfathers and great-grandmothers, regardless of their level of education, poetry (read, written, or spoken aloud) was an important outlet for their feelings and ideas. The enjoyment and writing of poetry was not confined to an academic elite. In Victoria's most widely circulated dailies, the *Times* and the *Colonist*, the verse of poets employed as book-keepers, bureaucrats and glassblowers was published.

Throughout Canada, in fact, public interest in reading and writing poetry seems to have peaked in the early years of the last century and not only among the well-educated classes. The great increase in literacy in the late nineteenth century, due to the expansion of compulsory primary education, meant that a large group of literate readers and listeners existed. As well, Mechanics'

Institutes and public libraries had inculcated a respect for literature among the general public which has never since been equalled. Of course, an upper class education (in the Greek and Latin classics) would help the reader to appreciate some of the more arcane published verse with its references to the legends, history and literature of the ancient world.

As well, with the development of typesetting machines and high-speed steam-powered presses, the production of daily and weekly newspapers was becoming mechanized. In Canada, between Confederation (1867) and the outbreak of the Great War (1914), newspaper circulation increased more than threefold. In these publications, hometown readers read local poets with special pleasure because they often expressed what was on many residents' minds. Even when the writers were not local persons, newspaper editors printed their poems when they thought the sentiment expressed therein was relevant to the hometown community and its attitudes, values, and problems.

These factors were magnified in Victoria. As early as the 1860s, verse was published regularly by early Victoria newspapers and journals. The short-lived *Victoria Daily Press,* which was published between 19 March and 16 October 1862, offered a poem in nearly every edition. From their inception in 1858 and 1884, respectively, the *Victoria Daily Colonist* and the *Victoria Daily* Times (amalgamated since 1980 as the *Times-Colonist*) regularly published poetry by locals and non-Victorians as well as by well-known British, American and Canadian writers. In 1864, the *Colonist* allotted a long column on page three to verse — and this in editions which usually ran to only four pages in total. The local labour union periodical, the *Semi-Weekly Tribune,* was committed to social and political reform, but its editors also expressed their enjoyment of poetry, "aesthetic" as well as polemical, offering several poems in every edition. The *B.C. Workman,* judging at least from the few extant 1899 issues, also offered poetry. (Its offerings were usually polemical.)

On 5 June 1884, the *Colonist* announced a policy of promoting local poets' works. Indeed, both the *Colonist* and the *Times* fostered local writers more than did other local nineteenth century newspapers such as the *Standard* or the *Evening Express.* Yet even these and other short-lived periodicals presented more verse than does any Victoria newspaper or journal today or any Vancouver newspaper then. For example, in several editions in 1893, the *Victoria Home Journal* featured poetry in a section, "Bad Rhyme, Good Reason", and later "Local Topics in Rhyme". At this time, both the *Times* and the *Colonist* occasionally featured poetry on their front pages. Inside, often two or three poems would appear in one edition. Those printed on the editorial page expressed the opinion of the editors or supported views those editors wished their readers to hold. Significant poems were published inside a frame, drawing attention to their themes. By the end of the nineteenth century, both these two dailies published the equivalent of a "poem of the day". For several years, in the early twentieth century, "Among the Poets" was a weekend feature of the

Colonist — although no local writers were presented. In 1906, the newspaper introduced a new column, "An Hour with the Editor" which included "current verse". In the 'teens, poems were regularly offered in the daily column, "In the Woman's Realm", edited by Maria Lawson ((1855-1943). In 1913, the *Times* introduced "A Line o' Cheer Each Day o' the Year". Beginning in 1903, the newspaper published once a week a column, "Jetsam, Jokes and Jingles". On weekends c. 1905, the *Times* offered "The Den" wherein poems, usually political, were published by "the Denizen". In September 1917, the *Colonist* introduced a weekly feature, "Men, Women, and Events" which usually included poetry.

The newspapers also published quasi-learned articles about poetry. In 1907, for example, the *Colonist* offered detailed comment on Canada's Charles G.D. Roberts (1860-1943) and in 1908 on the popular British imperialist poet, Rudyard Kipling (1865-1936). As the twentieth century dawned, the themes of published verse were similar to those long popular across the English-speaking world of the nineteenth century: love, death, children, religious faith, nature, landscape, humour, and politics. Poems for children and for women were featured more frequently.

Charles Swayne, who began employment at the *Colonist* in 1909 and was editor-in-chief from 1917 to his death in 1943, had a particular interest in literature and the arts, a fact which may account for the greater prevalence of poetry in that newspaper, compared to the *Times.* Assuming (I believe correctly) that many of its readers were familiar with Shakespeare, the *Colonist* used passages from his works to satirize current provincial politics. This practice began even before Swayne's time. For example, in 1867, in order to take a dig at local politicians, one of the newspaper's editors used "The Merchant of Venice" to make not entirely flattering references to local worthies such as Roderick Finlayson, Henry Crease and Governor Frederick Seymour. (*Colonist,* 4 March 1867) The *Colonist* also reproduced "Prologues" which were often written in blank verse for private amateur theatrical performances (as on 11 October 1871 and 14 August 1881). For example, at a performance of a "fine comedy, 'Naval Engagements'" at the Theatre Royal, an "exceedingly clever . . . amateur performance" to benefit the Mechanics' Institute, a typical "Prologue" (in rhyming couplets), was spoken by Lieutenant Sydney Eardley-Wilmot (1847-1929). It was "received with prolonged applause". (*Colonist*, 11 October, 1871)

Finding the first local poet to appear in a Victoria newspaper or periodical is difficult. The use of pseudonyms, for example, sets up an impenetrable barrier to the historian. Possibly the first poem by a local author on a Victoria subject, however, appeared on page one in the *Victoria Gazette* on 8 January 1859. The writer claimed to be "Augustine" and his/her work appeared in an editorial "City of the Dead", a critique of the Church Hill cemetery, which inspired in the editorial writer "dreariness, desolation, and gloom". Because a graveyard should be "rural and attractive", the editor urged the city to buy some rural acreage for a proper cemetery and quoted "**Augustine**":

Where forest trees their cooling shade
O'er mossy carpet's spread,
There nature hath her garden made,
And there should rest the dead;
There living pilgrims linger near

Where spirits vigils keep,
And mould the earth, or weep a tear
For those who dreamless sleep,
With warblers join in nature's hymn,
And sing their glorious requiem.

For our purposes, "Augustine" encapsulates the attitude of our mid-nineteenth century forebears towards nature (a healing, benign force) and death (a pleasant sleep). At it turned out, Ross Bay Cemetery was not opened until 1873 but its original appearance might have been just as "dreary, desolate, and gloomy" as the Church Hill graveyard because it was a stretch of barren countryside. Trees and shrubs were planted in the 1930s, with something of the result that would have pleased "Augustine".

The first bard whom I can identify as local is **Thomas Conlon**, with a poem entitled "Beacon Hill", in the *Colonist* on 19 March 1868. A long rambling epos, too long to reprint here, it typically praises the natural beauty of Victoria, lauding Foul and Ross Bays, the Gorge and more outlying areas such as Mount Tolmie, Mount "Cedar" (now Mount Douglas, originally Cedar Hill), Goldstream and Langford Lake. The *Times,* founded in 1884, was slower to accept local writers but by the later 1890s Janet K. Campbell and J. Gordon Smith were regular contributors from Victoria.

By this time, a readership for such poems had long existed. The Hudson's Bay Company officials and later emigrants from Britain exhibited a high level of literacy. Appointees to government positions here were selected partly on the basis of their education level, in a system that favoured degrees from Oxford or Cambridge University. A review of commercial establishments alone shows that many nineteenth century Victoria people enjoyed reading, including novels, drama and poetry and articles about current events. Less than twenty years after the HBC fort was founded, several newspapers served Victoria. As early as 1858, Thomas Hibben had established a stationery and book store. In 1864, David Spencer opened his reading room and bookstore. Some early Victorians owned large libraries, such as Benjamin William Pearse, surveyor-general of the Colony of Vancouver Island. Walter Colquhoun Grant, another early surveyor, arrived in 1849 with his large personal book collection. By the 1880s, Victoria had seen the establishment of a Shakespeare Club and the Alexandra Club for the enjoyment of music, art, and literature.

From the city's beginnings, education and its product, literacy, were important to Victoria citizens. On the outskirts of the city, Craigflower School, considered the first Canadian school built west of the Great Lakes, was founded in 1854. In 1860, a "Girls' Collegiate School" was established by the Anglican authorities. In 1865 a board of education was established and the beginnings of a public school system.* In 1886, the Provincial Museum was opened. In 1891 the Public (Carnegie) Library was established and, when Victoria College was founded in 1902, a campaign to have a local university was inaugurated. In 1911, construction began on a new four-storey high school, which became one of the most imposing structures in the community. In 1914, the Normal School for the training of teachers opened in an impressive towered structure on a rise overlooking the city (now Camosun College).

---

* British Columbia made public school attendance free in 1872 and compulsory in 1873.

Although we may be surprised at the virulence of some of the political verse, newspapermen would not publish anything exceptionally scurrilous or particularly bad by the standards of the time. Those poems which were published, however, tell us what editors thought was significant or worthy of being published in Victoria; hence we have an opportunity to consider the aesthetic taste of the era and the contemporary concerns of Victorians.

The foregoing may help to explain why our nineteenth century forebears loved to write, read, and hear verse. However, one more vitally important factor determined their interest in poetry. They lived in a city whose physical beauty inspired artists and writers. In fact, some called it "paradise".

PART TWO

A Perfect British Eden

PARADISE (AND ITS DISC0NTENTS)

When Hudson's Bay Company Factor James Douglas landed at Clover Point in 1842, he described the future site of Victoria as a "perfect Eden."* Since then writers of both prose and poetry have compared Victoria to "paradise". For example, Eustace Alvanley **Jenns** (1860 -1930) was an English immigrant who attended Victoria's Collegiate Institute and later practiced law in Vancouver. He imagined a protected island idyll in

VICTORIA

A fairy city, nestling in the hills
Surrounded by an azure ring of sea,
Where with her utmost beauty nature fills
The soul: where'er the eye may turn, there she
In wild magnificence and grandeur, wills
Her glory spread in mount and wave and sea.
That man might in her loveliness be blest,
And weary souls turn from their toil and rest.
Fair spreads the town; below the harbor lies;

---

* G.P. de T. Glazebroook (ed.). *The Hargrave Correspondence, 1821-43.* Toronto: The Champlain Society, 1938, 420; he "delighted in ranging over fields knee deep in clover, tall grasses and ferns reaching above our heads, at these uniquivocal proofs of fertility. Not a mosquitoe that plague of plagues did we feel, nor meet with molestation from the natives. (421)

Above, the woods and pleasant, fruitful plain;
Towards the north, the rocky hills arise,
Clothed with great firs, which tempest-tost in
vain,
Heave up their storm-grown trunks athwart the skies,
Nurtured with summer's heat and winter's rain.
And all around the boundless seas enclose
The isle to keep this jewel from her foes.

Far to the south, in the dim distance blue
Are mighty mounts, clad with eternal snow;
Clear in the summer air they rise to view,
Brilliant in sunshine, purple when the glow
Of sunset deepens to the darker hue
Of twilight, as the eve advances slow,
And fading altogether from our sight
When the ten million stars shine forth at night.

Who might not dream that this was Paradise
Lying in sunshine when birds lightly sing?
Where to the flower the hummingbird lightly flies
And trees give forth fresh verdure in the spring—
In summertime — or e'en when winter hies
Hither with snowflakes, and the steel skates ring;
Swift gliding o'er the frozen-breasted lake,
And laughing voices woodland echoes wake.

Hail then, ye mighty hills and forest deep;
Hail to the roaring deep, the babbling wave;

Fig. 4 Outpost of Empire: Cover of a tourist brochure, combining the natural abundance of paradise with the proud presence of the Imperial Navy at Esquimalt. The gorgeous local scenery of mountains, forests, and the Salish Sea is also suggested. (Victoria Tourist Association pamphlet)

Hail, ye calm heights on which the sunbeams sleep
And rocky shores, where rippling billows lave;
Hail, ye dark streams, where silvery fishes leap.
No greater beauty have I power to crave —
Here will I dwell amidst the light and flowers,
And pass in dreamy ease the peaceful hours.

(*Orpheus and Eurydice and other Poems*. Vancouver, 1910.)

Jenns' Victoria, although a relatively isolated "Eden", was not a tropical "jewel", for heavy snowfall was not uncommon. (See Joey Gosse's poem below.)

Since Douglas' time, poets have regularly lauded the city as a kind of "paradise". Writing much later than Jenns, **Dorothy E. Abraham** (1895-1990), of Faithful Street in Victoria, was only one of these:

This lovely Island set in a western sea,
A Paradise with mountains, verdant tree,
Of flaming sunsets, peaks, eternal snow,
And happy homes, where fire-lit faces glow.

In peaceful beauty unsurpassed it stands,
Its foam-swept beaches, miles of golden sand,
Lapped by the sea, a garden of the West,
A Gem of Loveliness where men find rest.

(*Romantic Vancouver Island: Victoria Yesterday and Today*, Victoria: Acme Press, 1947.)

When Jenns described how "all around the boundless seas enclose/ The isle to keep this jewel from her foes", we meet the sense that Victoria existed in a secure isolation protected from the rest of the world. The artist Emily Carr wrote of how, standing on Beacon Hill, "You forget all about Asia and Europe and Africa and the rest, and the wars and famines and earthquakes."* The poets echo this perception.

Before the Canadian Pacific Railway was built, however, to get to Paradise, you had to pass through Hell. In 1866, an anonymous traveller wrote this lamentation:

Original Ditty by a Victim

O listen all ye tempted, in search of land or gold,
Believing each delusive tale by shipping agents told
Of practical enjoyment, and every sort of ease,
Ensured on all their vessels in the very worst of seas.
For your own sake, example take,
My counsel do not shun;
And pause awhile before you make
A voyage round Cape Horn.

Australian vessels nowadays, fastidious tastes may please,
And liners to America are floating palaces;
East India and China ships would make a landsman stare;
But a voyage to Vancouver's land's a different affair.

---

* *Hundreds and Thousands. The Journals of an Artist,* in *The Compete Writings of Emily Carr*, Vancouver: Douglas & McIntyre, 1993, 785.

My simple story do not doubt;
Or you'll have cause to mourn
The blind belief that took you out,
To westward of Cape Horn.

We sailed, a merry company, enjoyed our wine and grog;
Sometimes we grumbled at our fare, and sometimes praised our prog;
Played cards and drafts, and when we found such light amusements vain,
We quarrelled then among ourselves, and made it up again.
At times afar, came down a spar,
Perchance a little worn;
But still we felt but little care
For dangers off Cape Horn.

Our Skipper was a smart one — his officers also;
The crew, though short, as fair a lot as other ships could show;
We quickly gained by Providence, calm seas and breezes fine,
A few degrees of latitude to southward of the line;
And there my eyes! The seas did rise,
As we were madly borne
Toward our fatal destinies,
The terrible Cape Horn.

By one rude pitch from out our beds we bolted in a breath,
And what we fondly term'd our berth had nearly
proved our death.
Chairs, tables, glasses, cups, and mugs around us soon
did fall,
And there we lay a helpless mass, the victims of the squall.
When we arose and gained our toes
Up in the air was borne,
One deep, yet hearty curse on those
Who brought us to Cape Horn.

Biscuits and butter, cakes and rolls, were mingled in a
mess,
Pickles and mustard, pork and cheese, and flasks of bitter
Bass.
Yet not one single article was ever at command,
And the one thing we wanted most, would never come to
hand.
In showers the bread flew round our head,
You really might have sworn
That all the victuals had a dread
Of going round Cape Horn.

And not alone did Christian men, this fatal influence feel.
The very animals themselves began to roll and reel,
The cats abandoned all the rats, and fed on their own tails,
The rabbits nibbled rope yarns, tin cans and copper
nails,
The pigs refused their scanty food,

And grunted all forlorn,
Finding all other language rude
To typify Cape Horn.

For six long weeks we tossed about without an hours' relief,
Our food impenetrable dough, and self-baptized beef;
Excepting when our cook vouchsafed to make an extra dash.
With some mysterious condiment denominated "ash".
Midst damp and fleas, and dirt and peas,
Of every comfort shorn,
I lay as bilious as you please
Whilst passing round Cape Horn.

Should even the tempestuous wind some moments cease to blow;
Down came a cataract of sleet, or avalanche of snow,
A pipe no longer cheer'd our lips, e'en brandy charm'd no more,
And those who stupid were, became more stupid than before.
Perpetual motion was the rule,
And could be better borne
Than what I suffer'd like a fool,
In going round Cape Horn.

And now I've quite exhausted all description to the dregs,
And language has become to me as useless as my legs.

My ribs are sore, and every limb almost superfluous feels,
And even my poor head is just as useless as my heels,
But this I know where ere I go,
As sure as I am born,
No gains again, or winds that blow,
Shall take me round Cape Horn.

(*Victoria Gazette,* 17 February 1860)

And when, in the 1860s, you finally disembarked in Victoria, "**Anonymous**" found:

Wretched streets and wooden buildings,
Without ornament or gildings,
Filled with folks of tempers various,
Driving on through life precarious.
Parsons, doctors, saints and sinners,
Broken merchants, new beginners,
Zealous bigots and free-thinkers,
Cobblers, shoemakers, and tinkers,
Poverty in shining slippers,
Churchmen, Methodists, and Dippers,
Wholesale dealers, loafers, peddlers,
Masons, carpenters, and saddlers;
Gentlemen with powdered wigs,
Coaches, wheel-barrows, and gigs,
Empty fops, more fools than wise men,
Bailiffs, lawyers, here you'll find them;
Many a beau without a penny,

Old gals and drunkards many,
Everyone his trade pursuing,
Home to wealth and some to ruin;
Prime coat shops for ready cash
Selling out their lie by trash;
Many a bargain if you will but strike it,
This is Victoria, how do you like it?

(*Colonist*, 4 November 1865)

At this time, the colony was in an economic slump as the gold boom had subsided.

Forty years later, problems with the streets remained and "**Anonymous**" pleaded:

The Carts, Please

Up from the busy city
And from the noisy street
Wherein the walls of brick and stone
Resound with tramp of feet,
There comes a wail of anguish
From the breaking civic heart —
"Oh, Fathers of the city,
Send us a watering cart."

The joyous idle zephyr
Swirls up the blinding dust,
While grimed and choked, the citizens

Bow low before each gust,
And you may hear their murmur
Beneath their broken sobs,
"Oh lay this dust, ye aldermen,
Or else give up your jobs."

Fig. 5 Queen Victoria (reigned 1837-1901): the Queen of Canada and Empress of India is said to have remarked to the telling of a ribald story, "we are not amused" which has lead some to conclude that 19th century people were stuffy. Judging from the cartoons, caricatures and poems published in the monarch's namesake city, however, they did indeed have a sense of humour, often expressed at the expense of public figures. (*Victoria Daily Colonist*, 16 October 1896)

"Our purple and fine linen
Is coated thick", they say,
"Our new black hats are yellow
Our new green suits are gray.
The tourist is upon us
With the summer dust and heart—
Oh Fathers of the city,
Aren't you going to clean the street?"

(*Colonist*, 29 May 1902)

Apart from the streets, certain other places in Victoria were less than salubrious, according to **A.E. Goodman** (b. 1880):

Suspect's Dream No. 2

I read the papers through the other night,
When drowsiness o'ertook me, but in spite
Of listless limbs I found myself in fright –
On James Bay Flats.

I saw huge parasites uncanny creep
Along the surface of a noisome keep,
While microbes, big as muskrats, sport and leap
About their wake.

A mammoth Entozoa whiles the time
By snoring loudly on the banks of slime
Dreaming of some more leprous putrid clime

More dank – more foul.

A giant polly-wig lies overfed,
Lashing with furious tail his muddy bed,
Then smiles a bilious smile and soaks his head
In mud and mire.

The putrifying sink, just as the air
Is, filled with scabies vulgaris
Oh, shades of Argyle from those pests pray spare us
Inflamed cuticles.

Trichinae spirales fall like rain
About me and I try to flee in vain –
But stay, where am I, I'm awake again
And have been dreaming.

(*Colonist,* 16 October 1892)

Soap-making refuse, wood chips, dead animals discarded into James Bay gave rise to a pungent stink. Since 1908, however, the Empress Hotel has stood on the site of the Flats.

Elsewhere in the area, other senses could be pleased. Meadowlarks — not native to southern Vancouver Island —were first released here in 1886; skylarks, in 1903. Several "odes" to larks were published in Victoria. These birds added to the "paradisal" atmosphere in parts of the city, providing almost spiritual comfort to the anonymous poet who wrote in the *Colonist* in 1907:

Ode to the Skylark

Old Friend in a new land
Pour your thrilling lay.
Sing on with glad heart
Making the world so gay.

Bring back memories
Touching forgotten strings.
Call up faces,
Hallowed ethereal things.

Old friends greet you
Gazing aloft as of yore
Greet you in silence
Entranced by the notes you pour.

(*Colonist,* 23 June 1907)

On the other hand, certain birds were not welcome. In 1914, "**The Bar(re)d**", a resident of Oak Bay wrote:

The Early Crocus

From fair Oak Bay
And far away,
The fountain pens make furious play,
Almost enough to choke us;
We wake at dawn

Our chickens gone,
While lightly from a neighboring lawn
Leaps forth the early crow-cuss.

We purchased larks
For groves and parks,
And if you'll pardon slang remarks,
The outlay nearly "broke" us;
But what's the use
To introduce
Sweet songsters, when from fir and spruce
Leaps forth the early crow-cuss?

In mornings hush
Erstwhile the thrush,
With some melodious, lilting gush
Of matin song, awoke us;
But Oak Bay
Views dawning grey,
Through discords harsh, as with his prey
Leaps forth the early crow-cuss.

(*Colonist*, 8 March 1914)

The wild vegetation of Victoria's environs was often praised. **Dudley Anderson** (1879-1945), described as a teacher and "private tutor" and a frequent contributor of poems to both the *Times* and the *Colonist,* took a position which would be considered controversial today:

The Yellow Broom

All hail to thee, thou yellow broom!
Thy softly waving amber bloom
Is our delight and glory;
Whene'er our city's fame we sing,
Thy golden branches we would bring
To weave into our story.

By waysides and in gardens fair,
In woods, and fields, and everywhere
I see thy splendor springing;
While on the green-clad hilltops grow
Like many a fair fashioned cloud
Thy wealth of beauty's clinging.
[and three more verses]

(*Times,* 24 June 1913)

First brought to the Victoria area c. 1850 by Captain Colquhoun Grant, the Scotch broom is now considered an "invasive species" and efforts are underway to extirpate it. In 1900 and again in 1907, the city fathers were already considering destroying the golden broom, but **L.A. Anderson** urged them to

Spare the Broom

Prithee, Council, spare the broom,
Touch not its beauteous spray.
This fair city is my home

And I feign would with you stay.

If an eyesore to a few
I'm sure in no one's way
Let them not influence you,
My enemies at Oak Bay.

My earth born ties ne'er sever,
To trim is far the best;
To hew me down forever,
Will not citizens protest? . . .

(*Colonist*, 25 October 1900 and *Colonist*, 15 June 1907)

Many poets praised Victoria's climate, occasionally echoing the American writer who found that "even the climate is British — mist and a warm slow rain."* Some found even the gray days of winter pleasant. **Charles L. Armstrong** (1884-1926), one of Victoria's most-published poets in the pre-war years — and during the war as a soldier-poet as well — enjoyed being

In the Rain

Oh, the fresh smell of winter rains that blow
Down the sea border of the Dallas Road;
Where lovely thoughts and wholesome fancies grow
And laggard spirits quicken to the goad.

---

* John Burroughs, quoted in Robin Ward, *Echoes of Empire. Victoria and its Remarkable Buildings*. Madeira Park: Harbour, 1996, xv.

Pain vanishes as swinging, on I go,
Beneath the spell now lighter grows the load.
Oh, the fresh smell of winter rains that blow
Down the sea border of the Dallas Road.

Wide are the windows of my mind's abode
Cleared by cold kisses from the mountains'
snow!
Rain in my face! my heart, it kens the code!
Rain in my eyes! — the only tears they know,
Oh, the fresh smell of winter rains that blow
Down the sea border of the Dallas Road!

(*Colonist,* 5 February 1911)

Of course, whether or not you appreciated Victoria's wet days depended on your accommodation. **Douglas B. Shepherd** (b.1896), a young journalist and Rifleman in the 289th Battalion, Canadian Rifles, from Windsor, Ontario, was billeted in a tent on the Willows Fairgrounds in 1918, and made this

Query from the Recruit

We like your charming city
On this soft Pacific slope,
When our Eastern snap is over,
We'll come again, we hope.
We love your snow-capped mountains,
Each city, street and lane,

But tell me, some old resident,
Does it always, always, rain?

The soldier from the eastland
You've received with open arms,
Till we, though bound for Russian snows
Forget the war's alarms.
We're in the Golden West now,
And we're awfully glad we came,
But tell me, some old-timer,
Does it always, always, rain?

Your climate's not so very bad,
It might be worse, we know;
We might be freezing in our tents,
And drilling in the snow.
But e'er we leave we'd like to see
The sunshine once again,
So tell me please, and tell me now,
Does it always, always, rain?

P.S. Dear Mr. Editor, — I would make this a lot longer but the sheet anchor of my tent is adrift and we are going full speed for Fort Street with breakers ahead.

(*Times,* 14 December 1918)

Shepherd was part of the Siberian Expeditionary Force on their way to attack the Russian Bolsheviks.

Actually, it didn't "always rain", but **Josh Wink** described aspects of Victoria's climate well:

<u>A Day in March</u>

Give me my big umbrella,
My heavy overcoat,
My rubber boots; my thickest scarf
To wrap about by throat;
My linen duster, also –
Be sure to think of that –
Likewise my suit of summer serge
And lightest weight straw hat.

At 6 a.m.
The sun is out
At 7 comes
A water spout,
At 8 the air
Will colder grow
At 9 we have
A heavy snow.
At 10 it's a warm
With summer breeze
11 brings
A frost and freeze,
At 12 o'clock
We go to lunch

With all this weather
In a bunch.

No, give me all the clothing
I'm lucky to possess,
And keep your eye upon my path
For signals of distress.
For in this chopped up weather
We soak and freeze and parch
And no man knows what's due to come
An afternoon in March.

(*Times,* 29 March 1901)

I cannot find any reference to Mr. Wink in the local records, but the *Times* editors obviously believed that his complaint applied to Victoria's climate.

A possible consequence of these weather conditions was described by one anonymous bard:

A Victim's Plaint

I've a horrible cold in my head,
And my eyes with rheum are sore
My nose is both tender and raw –
Such a cold I ne'er had before.

At night when I lie down to sleep
'Tis in vain I try to get rest.

For at once I start up with a cough
And a violent pain in the chest.

My head with pain is nigh burst,
Through lack of rest I'm quite lean;
I sneeze and I cough and I wheeze
And I feel most decidedly mean.

I've swallowed cod-liver oil
And horrible balsam and balm,
With divers concoctions and pills,
All warranted "to work like a charm".

I've dosed with "sure cures" till I'm sick,
And I'm quite as bad off as at first;
"Be patient" is easy to say,
But I'm afraid I sometimes have cursed.

This terrible nasty mean cold,
That makes one feel sick when he ain't;
'Twould try the patience of Job
And break up the smile of a saint.

Still one thing makes me feel glad
Although it isn't much news,
But in any part of the town
You can hear them all nosing kerchews!

(*Colonist,* 30 January 1887)

Victoria's proximity to the wilderness was often a theme, in particular for **Frederic Philips** (1862-1947), an English immigrant, probably a draughtsman living on Hillside Avenue. He gently mocked Victoria's image as a "city of gardens":

The Pioneer in Town

Yes, I may envy them their trim-kept lawns,
Their hollyhocks that proudly line the walks,
And roses trailing up the balcony
All in the English style.
And twirling water in a diamond spray,
To keep the grass green through the droughty days.

These townsmen have a knack of smug content.
But they can never drink the wine of life,
To tramp all day in endless forest glades,
Where sunshine comes in showers to refresh
The parched gloom of countless evergreens,
Or trace the piercing spire of some tall fir
Up to the zenith. Or at noon to lie
Beneath a cedar whose vast hollow bole
Would take ten men to circle . . .

No kingdom like a clearing in the woods.
The blue smoke of smouldering alder, new turned earth.
Incense to offer to the Lord of all.
There one is king indeed. Not ruling men—

That implies servitude on someone's part,
And servitude debases him who's served —
But guiding Nature's force, turning her laws
Into your channels. That indeed's to rule.

(*Verses from a Western Isle*, c. 1909)

Levi Houghton, a Victoria poet who died here in 1918, imagined himself writing a letter to a friend, inviting him to visit British Columbia's capital. His style was typical of some popular verse of the time — pompous and inflated — but the poem is a catalog of things that locals and visitors admired about Victoria:

Canada's vast and myriad acres—
Central prairies wheat's domain—
Ancient cities of th'Atlantic, —
All have share in praises' strain.
But of thou, — Dominion's fairest,
Brightest, sceniest, beauteous spot,
Those who chant of other places,
They are they who know thee not.
VICTORIA!
Honoured name on British tongue,—
She who dignified the Throne,
Left a name, 'twill last as long,
Long as thou dost bear her own!
City thou,— Dominion's Queen,
Regal true in Nature's splendor;
None like thee can e'er be seen,—

None can say I'll mend her.
VICTORIA!
England's beauty know so wide;
(Surely thou art England's sister-twin,)
Truly thou art dignified,
Fair without and fair within!
Old Ocean laps thy numerous Bays,
Bright Sol bedecks thy Parks,
With emerald green thy winding ways,
Call forth extolled remarks!
VICTORIA!
Rocky headlands, sandy beaches'
Mounts aspire to meet the sun;
Nature loving thou dost teach us,
Whilst we round with motors run,
Gnarled old oaks and Douglas pine [sic],
Gardens grand delights our fill
But who can yet compare design,
With the broom on Beacon Hill!
VICTORIA!
O'er the Straits of Juan de Fuca,
Olympic stately mountains see,—
Delighting visiting onlooker,
And he hails the sight with glee!
Cousin Sam's in thousands coming
Year by year to see thy glory,
And he ne'er forgets his roaming,—
Tells abroad thy wond'rous story!
VICTORIA!

For 'round thee he's been a-hunting
Cougar, bear, and deer and moose,
Likewise also gone a-fishing,
All his business cares cut loose.
Oak Bay Links and those of Colwood
Reached he these by street-car ride;
Boating, bathing, tennis, billiard,
All these pleasures, — more beside!
VICTORIA!
Mild's the clime, and summer not too hot,
'Tis minus Zero on the prairie;
Come and visit this blest spot.
Come yourself and bring dear Mary.
Come in Winter, come in Spring,
Come in Summer, Autumn too,
And when you come this song you'll sing:
"Victoria the whole year through!"
VICTORIA!

(Levi Houghton. *Victoria the Beautiful*, 1917)

Reading these verses and many of the ones that follow in this book, one can have the impression that some Victorians fell themselves to be happily isolated from the affairs of Europe and its power struggles. Despite changing social mores and technological developments, despite the tensions with Russia c. 1880 and the South African War (1899-1902), until 1914 many Victorians could insolate themselves in the view that their Vancouver Island "Eden" was akin to a remote tropical isle of easeful bliss. Even so, as Houghton's ode suggests, the British connection mattered very much to them.

ENGLAND'S SISTER-TWIN

Such was Levi Houghton's sobriquet for Victoria — and with some cause. By the end of the nineteenth century, most of Victoria's social, professional, business and political leaders hailed from Britain. Their nostalgia for the "Old Country" occasionally led to their giving their homes names redolent of British places. The banker Alexander Green and his wife Theophila, for example, called their new Rockland mansion "Gyppeswyk", Old English for Ipswich in Suffolk, where they had married. **M.E. Allen**, a Member of the British Columbia Legislative Assembly, declared at a St. George's Day dinner in Victoria in 1888:

My ancestors were Englishmen, an Englishman am I,
And 'tis my boast that I was born beneath a British sky.
I prize my peerless birthplace, for its freedom and its fame;
In it my father lived and died,-- I hope to do the same.
I've heard of foreign countries that are very fair to see;
But England — dear old England— is quite fair enough for me.
And he that on its happy soil is not content to stay;
May leave it when he likes, and find a better where he may.

We may not have the mountains which some other lands may show;

Their sides adorned with vineyards, and their
summits crowned with snow.
We may not boast the grandeur or the melancholy grace
Which tells of Time's destroying hand, or war's
terrific trace.
But we have fertile valleys,
We have hills and dales and dells
Where peace and plenty smile around

Fig. 6 Craigdarroch Castle (built 1889): Robert Dunsmuir (1825-89), the coal baron, evidently wanted to live as a "laird o' the manor" in this commodious mansion on a twenty-eight acre rural estate, recalling one he may have seen in his native Scotland. Before Hollywood's Emerald City and Disneyland, the towers and turrets of Craigdarroch suggested a magical hilltop idyll, not English but at least British. (*West Shore Magazine*, 1889)

And sweet contentment dwells.
And we have cliffs that beetle o'er and battle with the spray
Of a thousand waves that roll around a shore as free as they.

There's not a sea that on its breast a hostile fleet can bear
But England's flag is seen to fly in stern defiance there.
There's not a clime, east, west, or south, but echoes with the fame
Of England's dauntless warriors, and rings with England's name.
Our ancient institutions and our good old English laws
Have wrong from e'en our fiercest foes their wonder and applause.
Oh his must be a coward's heart who would not make a stand
For altar, throne, for hearth and home in such a native land.

(*Colonist,* 27 April, 1888)

Despite Allen's commitment to a political life in BC, he wanted to return to die in "dear old England". This combination of arrogant imperialism with love of the "old country" was a common theme. In fact, Allen's verses suggest that some Victorians may have felt in exile on Vancouver Island. For example, **Clive Phillipps-Wolley** had lived for two decades away from Britain, settling in Victoria's suburban Oak Bay and later in North Cowichan, but he was prepared to "make a stand" in defence of his birthplace. In the

Colonist (21 July, 1910), part of one of his poems declared, "British are We":

When Britain's foemen meet,
We will not question if She's wrong or right —
At the first flap of that old flag — we fight . . .

English-born **Cecily Fox Smith** (1882-1954) who lived on Simcoe Street and worked as a secretary in Victoria, 1904-1913, evidently found herself in a kind of exile here:

The Long Road Home

There's a wind up and sighing along the waterside,
And we're homeward bound at last upon tonight's full
tide;
Round the world and back again is very far to roam—
And San Juan Strait to England, it's a long road home! . . .

The leaves that just are open now, they'll have to fade
and fall.
There'll be reaping time and threshing time and
ploughing time and all;
But we'll not see the harvestfields nor smell the
freshcut loam,
We'll be rolling gunwales under on the long road
home. . . .

And it's "home, dearie, home", when the anchor rattles
down
In the reek of good old Mersey fog, a rolling rich and
brown,—
Round the world and back again it's very far to roam,
And all the way to England it's a long road home!

(*Colonist*, 17 December 1912)

Fox Smith actually returned to England shortly before 1914. Presumably people like her wanted the Union Jack — not the Canadian Ensign — as Canada's flag. In 1887, one **anonymous** poet described in the *Colonist* "The Only Flag for Canada". His casual association of "freedom" or "liberty" (vaguely defined) with military predominance was common:

We want no flag but the old Red Cross!
The flag our fathers bore
On many a well-fought field of fame
In the glorious days of yore!
The flag that floated o'er the Nile
And at Trafalgar too;
And got a baptism of renown
On the field of Waterloo!

We want no flag but the old Red Cross!
That sprung from freedom's soil!
And fluttered high above the reach
Of hands that would despoil —
The gallant banner of the brave

Our country's Union Jack,
That never streamed above a slave,
Or swerved from glory's rack!

We want no flag but the old Red Cross!
The terror of the main
That never had its blazonry
Polluted by a stain.
The old and honored bunting—
The chosen of the free —
Which made our land for ages
The mistress of the sea!

We want no flag but the old Red Cross!
'Neath which our country grew
The mightiest empire of the earth,
To freedom ever true!
The emblem of high enterprise
And of the rights of man,
Which Liberty's disciples . . .

We want no flag but the old Red Cross!
For this young land of ours
To raise it to the standard
Of the world's mighty powers
We've flourished 'neath its sheltering folds
In darkness and in light;
Then give to us the good old flag
We claim it as a right!

(*Colonist,* 7 March 1887)

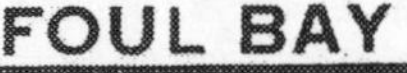

Fig. 7 A Tea Room Advertisement: The ostensible "Englishness" of Victoria, expressed frequently in poetry and tourist brochures, was also used to advertise local businesses. (*The Week*, 31 July 1909)

References to the Nile, Trafalgar and Waterloo recalled British victories over Napoleon and the French.

Such idealization of the “mother country” extended to the British Empire as well. **Earnest McGaffey** (1861-1941) dedicated these verses to Richard McBride, Premier of BC, in 1914:

While Britain Rules the Sea.

Now by the light of Nelson’s fame,
The soul of Francis Drake,
By bold Sir Walter Raleigh’s name
And Collingwood and Blake,
There is no need for British men
To ever bend the knee;
The sword is mightier than the pen
While Britain rules the sea.

From far Australia’s golden sands,
From Canada’s wide shores,
From India’s coral-crusted strands,
From London’s very doors
Once voice is heard, one cry goes back
Its echo sounding free
We’ll fly aloft the Union Jack
While Britain rules the sea.

(*Colonist*, 4 February 1914)

Note the reversal of the adage, “The pen is mightier than the sword.” Some Germans asked, “By what right does Britain ‘rule the sea’?”

The arrogance expressed in these verses is part of the background to the Great War of 1914-1918.

Imperial soldiers were heroes to some. **Ralf Sheldon-Williams** of Cowichan commemorated the death of Field Marshal Frederick Roberts (Lord Roberts) in 1914. The soldier had distinguished himself in the suppression of the Indian Mutiny (1857) and in Abyssinia, Afghanistan and the South African War. Sheldon-Williams' colourful and idealized imagery was welcomed in by many in Victoria and editors were happy to publish it.

The Passing of Bobs Badahur
(November 1914)

Hush! A Sahib goes by!
From Dover cliffs to far Cashmir
Rings the challenge, "Who goes there?"
Thrilling slumbering echoes round the path by which you go:
From Punjab plain to Calais pier
The echoes leap from days that were,
Fling the answer, bugle clear:
"Friend — who loved a foe!"
Rung-ho!
Rajah, nawab, seminar
Maharaj and mebetah
Lace with arched and lambent swords
The path by which you go.
From Rangoon up to Kandahar,
By palace stilled and hushed bazaar,

Your guard of honor flashes far,
For India loved you so . . .
By Bengal and Baluchistan,
By Bolan Pass and Radakahan,
An empire's manhood hails a man —
"Badahur, rung-ho!" . . .

(*Colonist,* 19 November 1915)

Of course, Indian opinion of "Bobs" may have been different.

Others admired the war-like qualities of the Empire's subjects. **Ralph Younghusband,** born in India in 1889, a Great War veteran, later resident in Duncan, dedicated these lines "With respect and admiration to [his kinsman] Lieut.-Col. Sir Francis Younghusband, KCIE, KCSI,* author, explorer, and soldier":

To India

Mother of warrior sons!
When the call went forth from the East,
Like ravens unto a feast
You sent them swift to the fray
Who know how to fight and pray
At home or under the guns.
Mother of warrior sons!
Who are turbaned, subtle and calm

* KCIE stands for Knight Commander of the Indian Empire; KCSI, for Knight Commander of the Star of the Order of India.

Full of the mystical charm
Of Shiva, Krishna and Brahm,
Who know that death is a gate
Opening to endless life!
They welcomed the hour of strife
And smiled at the stings of fate
Mother of warrior sons!

Sacred! Ancient on earth,
Filled with the glamour of things
That only the Orient brings
To students of occult lore!
Shall I stand 'neath thy palms once more
While the radiant sun doth set
Behind temple and minaret,
Where the throbbing tom-toms beat
And the patter of naked feet
On the glowing, golden sand
Tells that a pilgrim band
Answers the call to prayer?
Shall I ever go back over there,
To the heart of mother of sons?
Mother of Warrior Sons! . . .

(*Times,* 13 May 1918)

These lines would appeal to those Indian Army officers who, at the end of their careers or because of unrest in the subcontinent, had retired to southern Vancouver Island — and to their relatives and friends here.

And, of course, the monarchy itself was revered, often in vocabulary which would be considered excessive today. The death of Queen Victoria in 1901 saw an outburst of apparently genuine lamentation. **Frederic Irving Taylor,** probably a "stenographer", living on Pandora Avenue, wrote of her as the "mother" of the British Empire:

Victoria

What is this gloom that fills the air? — this shadow
o'er the earth?
Why seem the ocean waves asleep? Why hushed is
Nature's mirth?
The bells are tolling, tolling, and the solemn whispers
spread
From mouth to mouth, o'er every land,— "The Queen, —
the Queen is dead"!

Oh, the scepter now hath fallen from our Sovereign
mother's hand,
And the eye of Majesty hath lost the lustre of
command;
And the heart whose pulse responded to a mighty
empire's life
Is chilled at last and silent, — She is dead, the
mother, — wife.

She is dead, the Queen of Sovereigns; for each subject was a king;
The royal blood of liberty flowed from the purple spring,
And every vein was richer by the earth's most noble blood;—
The mother of an empire, an imperial brotherhood.

*Hers was the Koh-i-noor** *of crowns; her heritage was great*
But more she prized the virtues born in high or low estate;
Her womanhood was queenly, and the chosen of her race,
Less deemed she of ancestral crowns than Victoria's crown of grace.

The Sovereign of a century was numbered with the dead.
But Time, the leveler of all, spared yet that sacred head.
So might the passing era clasp the era newly born,.
For worthiest she to bless the night, and hail the rising morn.

Ah yet, the loss tho' grievous there is solace in our tears!.
She bequeaths a proud tradition to the unbegotten years;
And the mother of the infant in the ages yet to come

---

* The Koh-i-noor was, at this time, the largest known diamond in the world.

Oft will bless the Queen of Mothers, — royal mother of the home.

(*Colonist,* 23 January 1901, front page)
Elsewhere, Taylor eulogized the late queen as "holiest, best of mortals born to high estate". (*Times Royal Commemorative Number,* October 1901)

When the Prince of Wales (later King Edward VIII) visited Victoria in 1919, to lay the cornerstone for the pedestal of the Queen Victoria statue, one "**H.E.K.**" wrote:

Welcome!

We greet you, sir, Prince of the royal line,
Around whose youthful brows the laurels twine
Of gallant service, gladly done,
And even now our strongholds one by one
Are yielding, captive to that boyish grace
And honest, open, true born British face,
Sure pledge that in the days to come
Should bugle's blast, and rolling drum
Arouse once more the nation's might,
You'll play the man, for God and Right,
We greet you, sir, with joyous heart and voice,
The Empire's heritage, the Empire's choice!

(*Colonist,* 23 September 1919)

On the same occasion, the *Colonist* reproduced this poem by **Ruth Prinsep,*** in Victoria. Some of her reverence may be hard to understand today but the newspaper's editor evidently thought the sentiments expressed would find an echo in Victoria.

<u>To the Prince of Wales</u>

I would that I had danced with you, dear Prince
Upon one gala night
Not when Victoria crowded to the Ball [at the
Empress]
Oh! Not at all.
But when, in simple style
You danced awhile;
Then would have been the hour of my delight.

I would that I had kissed your hand, dear Prince.
But even that brief joy was not for me
Not one of those was I
Who, passing by,
Received your smile;
Charmed for the while

*Although the *Colonist* identifies this poet as living in Victoria in 1919, I can find no record of a "Ruth Prinsep" here. C. 1910, a woman with the same name was a British suffragette. Conceivably, she was visiting here.

By your fresh youth and frank simplicity

I would that I had kissed your face, dear Prince,
Not to show off my prowess to the crowd
Not for a bet
But yet . . .
The true expression of a subject's heart –
A loyal subject who takes no part
In the more intimate gatherings called for thee.

("Victoria, B.C. Sept. 27th, 1919": *Colonist,* 5 October 1919)

Clearly, prominent people of the United Kingdom and the Empire were revered in "British" Victoria but, in fact, the city's population never completely reflected the society of the "mother country".

PART THREE

Victorians and Others

AN ETHNIC MOSAIC

Even ignoring the Scottish, Welsh and Irish element in Victoria's population, the nineteenth-century city was not quite "England's Sister-Twin" but was a melange of ethnicities, including Hawaiians, blacks, and Québecois, not to mention the Salish First Nation. Later came the Chinese, the Japanese and the Sikhs.*

As for the coastal natives, they were given to warfare and slave-taking but, after the arrival of the Europeans, they may very well have looked back on those pre-contact days as "paradisal", if not in the sense of James Douglas' "Eden". The Hudson's Bay Company and Christian missionaries regarded the Salish as little more than ignorant savages. Some sympathy for the native people and their decline, however, was occasionally expressed. **George Mason** (1827-1893) was an Anglican missionary who had served in Hawaii and Nanaimo. On October 28, 1875, he read the following poem (which he may have written himself) at the Victoria Mechanics' Institute:

Lo: The Poor Indian

Made in the image of his maker, — man
Howe'er degraded, yet reflects the plan
Original — as by the eternal mind

---

* Dr. John Lutz' on-line walking tour, "Imperial Paradise?", questions the "Britishness" of Victoria. (web.uvic.ca/walktour/index.html)

In archetypal beauty first designed;—
Of various feature, color, habit, all
Their primal birthright faithfully recall;—
The same in kind, tho' diff'ring in degree,
They form but one vast human family.

Why should the proud Caucasian scorn to own
His dusky brother of the torrid zone,
Or deem the fairer kin by right may claim
Superior station and a nobler name!
If, as we boast, the Anglo-Saxon race
Hold in the scale of nations foremost place
Be sure that He from whom the blessing flows
For some wise reason eminence bestows;—
And not to foster arrogance or pride
Doth the Omniscient His gifts divide
To every creature,— working as He will
Among the sons of men His purpose still. . . . .

Behold these squalid relics of the past,
Wrecks on Time's changeful billows drifting past,
Hope's future darken'd, self-reliance gone
They cower abash'd before the stranger's scorn;
Too low for vengeance, or with smother'd hate
His meaner vice they basely imitate;
Nor can the memory of their chieftain sires
Inflame the embers of their wonted fires.

A time there was, ere yet the white man's power
Had robbed the Indian of the rightful dower
Received from Heaven, through Nature's willing
hand,
To roam unchallenged down the rocky strand,
Or spear the salmon for his daily food:—
Or chase the red deer through the tangled wood . . .

Would God the historic page
In truth might trace a brighter, happier age
For the poor Indian, since the stranger came
And gave his native shores the foreign name.
Alas! The mournful muse recounts the tale
Of vice and misery with their deadly trail
Tracking their progress who were sent to bless
But only taught enlightened selfishness . . .

They brought . . . the madd'ning lust of gold,—
Worse than the rule idolatry of old.
They poured the intoxicating draughts of fire,
Enhanced the value of unchaste desire . . .

Lo! The poor Indian now! From street to street
In cast-off finery, with naked feet
Listlessly strolling object of contempt,—
His claims neglected, and his lands pre-empt,—
Despoiled, uncared for, destitute he roams,
A homeless exile, 'mid his native homes!

Or, like the leper, doom'd apart to dwell,
Making his Indian camp a shameless hell! . . .

Down o'er the distant hills there shoots a ray
Of brighter omen for the coming day.
There is a happy spot of busy life
Where order reigns,
Where hush'd the din of strife.
Harmonious brethren 'neath paternal rule
Ply their glad tasks in Methlacatla's school.
There Duncan holds supreme his peaceful throne
His power unquestioned, and their rights his own.
Anvil and hammer, saw and wheel resound,
And useful art of industry abound,
While faith and knowledge find an altar there
In "Learning's" hall and stately house of prayer. . . .

These are they whom Christian love can train,
Loos'ning the bands of Satan's deadly chain,—
And pouring on their souls the Gospel light,
Amid the darkness of their heathen night. . . .

(*Colonist*, 5 March 1893)

Methlacatla was a Christian settlement of Native people established by the Anglican minister William Duncan (1832-1918) in 1862 on the Skeena River near Prince Rupert. His program sought to isolate its inhabitants from white "civilization" in an economically self-sufficient community of fish canners, spinners, weavers and craftspeople, but ultimately sought to eradicate any vestiges of their culture.

Unlike the Salish, the blacks played a relatively integrated role in Victoria's growth. One of their leaders, Willis Bond (1825-1892), a storekeeper, contractor and "house mover", lived on View Street and inspired some clumsy, teasing, but evidently well-meant praise from "**An Admirer**":

Willis Bond

Willis Bond is Victoria's pride,
He has big feet and a colored hide.
His shoulders have a Grecian bend,
Which to his figure grace doth lend.

He is an orator by nature born,
Though by conflicting powers torn
Commercial Union is his forte
When helped by a glass of rare old port.

When on the lecture stage he stands
The landlord for his rent demands;
So then a collection is taken
And into his beaver the nickels are shaken.

Then in soft and musical tones,
Which jarred on his hearers' bones
He proceeded with his speech
Which acted like a leech.

Imperial Federation is another theme
Upon which he vents a little steam
And when the steam exhausted is
He says 'tis time to close his "bis".

Long, long life to Willis Bond,
Of whom learned men are all so fond.
When his last days are drawing nigh,
May his thoughts be of God most high.

(*Colonist,* 23 February 1890 [supplement])

We can't know if this poet was white or black but it is significant that the *Colonist* editors wanted to publish the verses — and on the front page of the Sunday Supplement. "Commercial Union" recommended a customs union between Canada and the United States. The concept of "Imperial Federation" would have involved a single federal state comprising the Dominions of the British Empire. Whether or not Bond favoured one or both of these is not clear. "His beaver" was his hat.

East Asians fared much less well politically and poetically in nineteenth century Victoria. The following lines were "Written for the *Colonist*" by "**S.**":

The Barbaric Curse

'Tis laughable though 'tis pitiful
As we shout till our throat is hoarse

To see our beautiful city full
Of the Heathen Chinese curse.

We rant and rave to prevent them
While under our very nose
As if the foul fiend had sent them,
They come with each wind that blows.

And now, what vile greed first taught them;
They practice with skillful hand.
Alas, for our fellow workmen
With such rivals in the land.

What a pity that all must suffer
For the gain of a grasping few
As this scum of barbarian gutter
Falls on us like pestilent dew.

We spread our hands in petition
To rulers, our children to save,
All in vain! Why, then, call it sedition
Should we chase them back over the wave.

(*Colonist,* 13 July 1882)

Just one of several virulent and offensive poems found in the early newspapers, such verses and their attitude are the background to the several exclusion acts and the notorious head tax. Needless to say, it is very unlikely that the Chinese thought of Victoria as "paradise".

Fig. 8 Amor de Cosmos ejects a Chinese man: the otherwise radical (by 19th century standards) editor and politician shared Victorians' dislike of the city's east Asian element. Ironically, as servants, business-owners and labourers, "paradise" could not have survived. *(Canadian Illustrated News,* 26 April 1879)

* * *

THE GREAT . . .
AND THE NOT SO GREAT

Victoria's poets lauded admired leaders, occasionally in unique ways. In 1877 this anonymous poem used the "acrostic" to praise the Hudson's Bay Company chief factor and governor of Vancouver Island and later of British Columbia. (Read the initials at the left.)

In Memory of Sir James Douglas

In peaceful slumber rests the honored Knight,
No shadow marks the Spirit's happy flight.
Muses shall praise, and with their lyres tun'd
Extoll his virtues from the earthly tomb.
Mingling in life, to all mankind a friend,
Obative kindness marked his life; the end
Recorded, leaves unsullied virtues fame,
Yielding in tears, to mourn an honor'd name.
Of him belov'd, the Province long may mourn;
Free from all pomp, to arrogance unborn,
Steadfast in truth a life thus noble spent
Inscribes alone a lasting monument.
Resolv'd to rule by what his will inclin'd
Justice declar'd what equity design'd;
Alike to all,— no potent power to move,—
Made might to conquer through respect and love.

Example mark'd, and what precept instill'd
Shap'd well the mould which he with honor fill'd.
Departed counsellor of sterling worth,
Of whom the title won, not left by birth;
Upon thy tomb, what "sculptor'd art" designs

Fig. 9 Premier Richard McBride: The long-serving premier of British Columbia in a more generous caricature, welcoming settlement in the province. (*Victoria Daily Times*, 11 January 1913)

Give place to title what REAL WORTH defines.
Let, then, the ashes lie, that 'neath the bust
Afford example which in memory must
Still live, though monument decay to dust.

("Victoria, August 9th, 1877", *Colonist,* 10 August 1877.)

Not every colonist or poet thought so highly of Douglas. (See below, James Deans' poem on Langford.)

In 1912 **Walter Howard** (1880-1966), a journalist living on Beach Drive in Victoria, in praising Premier Richard McBride, (served 1903-1915), described well the economy of BC a century ago and expressed the optimism of the times:

To the Honorable Richard McBride

On the Eve of his Election, the Commencement of his Third Term as Premier of the Province of British Columbia:

Child of the Western Land
Born in the Royal Town,
Hard by the timbered strand
Of Fraser, racing down,
How came those gifts of thine?
Imagination great,
With eloquence to shine,
Thy power to plan, create?
In childhood's tender years
A lad at work or play,

'Midst boyhood's hopes and fears
Couldst see the far-off day,
When, by the people's choice,
Their leader thou shouldst stand,
A MAN by manhood's voice,
To rule our own dear land?

Didst see the valleys peopled
By a stalwart farming breed?
Didst scan the cities' steeples
Didst watch the iron steed?
Didst hear the sledges ringing
As the drillers pierce the rock;
Didst hear the buzz-saw singing,
Where the lumber freighters dock?
Where the eagles soared secluded,
Where forests dimmed the light,
And foolish man deluded,
Had given up the fight.

But now oh youthful dreamer,
Thou modern Joseph, now,
Imaginative schemer,
We term thee, yea, and bow
Our heads in just obeisance
To one who, more than all,
Has proved his true allegiance
Has heard his country's call;
To open up her treasures,

To reach her hoarded wealth,
Fish, ore, or coal in measures,
Fruit, lumber, farms in tilth
Great is the debt we owe thee,
Vast is thy labour done,
Still Fair Columbia's glory
Shines on her honoured son!

(*The Week*, 23 March 1912)
The "Royal Town" was New Westminster, BC.

James Deans (1827-1905), a prolific Victoria poet, waxed enthusiastic over the visit of the Governor-General Lord Aberdeen and his wife, who served 1893-98.

A mighty crowd has gathered round; they cover wharf
and shore,
To give them such a welcome as was never known
before.
Noble steeds are prancing on the wharf, impatient of
delay,
All wary, watching, waiting, long to bear our chief away;
Now dimly o'er Gonzales hill a steamer's smoke is seen;
It bears our much-loved Governor, our noble Aberdeen.

He comes! he comes! Five thousand tongues the
joyful news proclaim;
They come! They come! The gathering crowds take
up the glad refrain;

Auld Scotia's sons in grand array with pipes and flags
they stand,
All come to welcome the great chief from Scotia's
fatherland . . .

(*Times,* 1 December 1894)

Deans reminds us that Victoria might well have been called "A Little Bit of Old Scotland".

Was the poet sycophantic? Naïve? Deluded? Perhaps. Somewhat less effulgent is a poem "written for the *Colonist*": **"H.E.K."** praised the retiring Lieutenant-Governor Sir Henri de Lotbinière (served 1900-1906), a "gentleman of France" who became very popular in Anglophilic Victoria:

Fare Thee Well!

Adieu, Sir Henri! You all hearts have won,
And here's a humble tribute to a setting sun
Which sinks in evening splendors, calm and bright,
And long will leave behind a gentle, lingering light:
The memory of a sunny smile, a kindly glance,
*And courtly bearing of a Gentleman of France,**
May favoring zephyrs waft you from the shore,
And all good guard you, till at length once more
You view the fair St. Lawrence, silver winding to the sea,
And tho' thousand miles, or more, will sever us from thee,

---

* De Lotbinière was born in Epernay, France, but lived much of his life in Québec.

Still we hope there'll hide within your heart a memory
of us yet,
Whilst we, who wish you now Godspeed, we never
can forget.

(*Colonist*, 27 May 1906)

In 1851, Edward Langford, an English immigrant, established himself as a gentleman farmer on a large property which he named Colwood. Bitterly at odds with the Hudson's Bay Company, Langford was forced to leave the colony in 1861. **James Deans** regretted his 1861 departure in a poem written in Scots dialect:

An Election Farce

Darkest and saddest days for our Colony
Strongly the storms of adversity Claw
Darkest of sable Clouds pregnant with villainy
Hangs ower our parlement, Langford's awa.

Devotees of beaver skins, down with monopoly
Musk rats and salt salmon, down with them aa
[You] *sic hearted God fearing on with your panoply*
Bring back the laddie the knaves sent awa.

Sae as we adore him, until they restore him
We'll hate the black Clique who has sent him awa . ..

(Reproduced in *Old Langford. An Illustrated History 1850 to 1950.* Victoria: Town and Gown, 2003.)

Amor de Cosmos (1825-1897), founder and editor of the *British Colonist*, an MLA, Premier and later an MP, was more often satirized than praised. He tried to convince the authorities to have the main line of the new Canadian Pacific Railway terminate in Victoria. Rumours circulated that he had "sold out" to John A. Macdonald, who reneged on his promise to extend the railway to BC's capital. Many here, including **"B.P."** were enraged:

Beware the Ides of March

The ides of March full well had fled
As through an eastern village sped
A note which, borne through wind and rain,
Had on superscription plain —
De Cosmos.

The delegate he saw the light
Of countless dollars shining bright:
Perchance an office might transpire!
Could more be found to raise the fire
Of A. De Cosmos?

Try not to pass, true prudence cried;
Conceit's no use, nor yet false pride.
Made answer he: "my time is past;
My pedigree will stand the last,
De Cosmos".

"Should failure come I can but rest
Upon Victoria's swasive breast,
And trap again her money-chest,
They little know the inner vest
Of A de Cosmos".

REFLECTIONS FOR VICTORIANS
[the poem continues]
Victorians, all full well you know
The vote De Cosmos gave;
Now, was he loyal, Was he true?
Or to his spleen a slave?

(*Colonist,* 12 July 1882)

In 1882, the provincial government granted twenty per cent of Vancouver Island, all mineral rights there and a subsidy of $750,000 to the Nanaimo coal baron, Robert Dunsmuir (1825-1889), so that his company could build a railway to be owned and operated by himself. The magnate was a member of the provincial government, a fact which led to the suspicion of corruption.

Provincial Anthem

(to the tune of "God Save the Queen")

I am King Grab, you see,
I own this country –
   I am King Grab.

Now my bridge is complete,
Mayor, Councillor en fete
Come grovel at my feet,
I am King Grab.

Hirelings! Come sing my praise!
Bulldoze Tom Humphreys,
And crush him down;
He's practiced honesty,
Hence comes his poverty;
Just the reverse with me,
I wear a crown.

And when I come to die
You need not wail or cry:
Yourselves console.
Know that I am to be
Throughout eternity
Where there's no scarcity
Or want of coal.

(*Times,* 4 April 1888)

Thomas Humphreys (1840 –1890) was an MLA. The "bridge" was the Johnson Street Bridge, carrying the new railway across the harbour into the town at Store Street.

Provincial bureaucrats did not escape poets' wrath, as in these verses, ostensibly written originally around 1867, when an ex-official of the colonial government lamented the dismissal (possibly politically motivated) of half a dozen government clerks. The *Times*, evidently thinking that was a subject was still relevant, printed it in 1891 and again in 1914.

Nothing New Under the Sun

When first I joined the official staff
A few short years ago,
How pleasantly we passed our time
None but ourselves can know.

The government was solvent then,
And ne'er had cause to rue
The payment of our salaries —
Tho' we had naught to do.

And thus we young official swells
Ne'er thought of future woe,
But passed the time in idleness,
A short time ago.

'Twas in the time of good Sir James
Those happy days were passed;
Tho' had we seen we might have known
They were too bright to last.
What little work we had to do
I knew was seldom done——
Tho' in each office there were three
To do the work of one. . . .

'Tis to De Cosmos we owe all—
Oh, how I hate that man.
Throughout the shabby mean campaign
He always led the van.
When I am working on the road,
Or floundering tho' the snow,
I'll curse him every breath I draw
And wish him down below.

And thus, etc.

(*Times,* 24 April 1891 and 12 December 1914)

In 1899, "**D.K.J**." believed that excessive conservatism was holding back Victoria's development and, fearing Vancouver's ascendence, he lambasted the city fathers:

The Mossbacks

Victoria's mossbacks are weeding [sic] *out fast*
So long as they're with us the dull times will last.
Many chances to boom our fair town has been given
They're no good for this earth, they should all be in heaven.

The fine harbor scheme that could thousands employ
Will be killed by amendments —"It's too big" they
will cry;
So leave things as they are no mill will we pay
We want no advancement — good enough is our day.

Mr. Shakespeare, that hero of railway connection,
Invited the Fifty to have an inspection
And declared at a meeting, 'twixt a wail and a weep
That for twenty long years they had all been asleep.

The C.P.R. scheme first on paper looked well.
Some heavenly power hath broken the spell
But the price asked by Dunsmuir made some
mossbacks sick,
They are all now quite well, but still ready to kick.

These old fogies are greedy, let me be understood.
They want something for nothing, and that something
good;
They should step up trade and their purse strings as well
'Twill bring crowds to our city, vacant lots we can sell.

We can outstrip Vancouver for we have the cash,
But they have the energy, pluck and fine dash;
So let us [illegible] *in one grand direction*
The harbor scheme first, then railway connection.

(*Times,* 30 May 1899)

The feisty tone here was typical of the *Times.* A sense of rivalry with Vancouver, the upstart city was widespread in "paradise". Dunsmuir's Esquimalt and Nanaimo Railway was supposed to assuage local ire, but evidently did not. Mr. Shakespeare was Mayor Noah in the 1880s. Ironically, had Victoria outstripped Vancouver in development, it would have lost much of the charm (and urban fabric) which made it "Edenic" to some and still does today.

Lesser folk were occasionally the subject of verses. Jabez King (1843-1918), for example, was a dairy farmer in the Fairfield area and sometime express delivery man. **Wellington J. Dowler** (1860-1927), city clerk and poet who lived on Cook Street, extolled him on his death in 1918:

Jabez King (in Memoriam)

"I've left some baggage at the dock, the C.P.R.'s front pier.
I want it brought to my address, you'll need the slips to 'clear'.
Tell them at home they'll find the checks to claim it in the hall
In the pocket of my overcoat that hangs there on the wall."

"Aye, aye, sir," Jabez answered straight, and cracked his whip with vim,
The old horse whisked his tail, forthwith, and ambled swift for him;
In twenty minutes more my trunk was landed at the door
And all the sundry luggage with it stacked upon the floor.

The time had come, the season ripe, to rear my summer camp;
I knew just where to pitch that tent away from din or damp;
On grassy knoll, in cooling shade, beneath a giant tree,

Whose roots are laved by crystal springs and steamlets,
by the sea.

And so I said to Jabez then, "I'll want your biggest van,
The one you use in summer time to carry all you can,
To shift my stuff to 'Dolcefarm' the spot where care
take wings,
These pots, and pans, and chairs, and beds and all the
other things."

I witness that I passed to him no other word that day.
E'er noon the morning afterward the whole was moved
away,
And, when the evening shadows fell, I hied me to the
stream,
The tent was up — the camp complete — I slept,
without a dream.

From morn till night, for forty years did Jabez drive
these streets;
Dame Fortune never pressed his lips with Joy's full
cup of sweets,
But friends and patrons, everywhere their ardent
faith instilled,
A trust committed to his hand would always be fulfilled.

They knew his horse might drop down dead, his dray
dissolve in wreck,

But Jabez, not a whit dismayed, would still be found "on deck";
That steamers might not dock on time, and inbound trains be late
But, when they came, they'd find him waiting, just outside the gate.

I've seen him touch his Derby hat, when waving his salute,
A smile would light his rugged face, although his lips were mute.
As deftly done as though he drove in high postilion state,
Instead of on a wagon-box, with "bronco" for his mate.

But few escape life's woes, among the lowly or the great;
A simple test of manhood is the way one meets his fate;
Some cry their troubles far afield, some curse, and others jest,
The way that Jabez had was this — he wrapt them in his breast.

He had a heart, has Jabez, aye, I found that out one day,
The sun was shining brightly down, as it had shone in May,
Two years ago, to "Willows Camp", my son's effects he bore,
Not knowing then, nor did we think, that he'd return no more.

A year passed by, again he [Jabez] *came, responding to a call,*
The direful word had come from France, that word was known to all,
The door-bell rang, but when he spoke — the sound was like a moan,
And, for my son, he wept great tears, as if he'd lost his own.[*]

The Doyen of the one-horse drays has passed, at last, to rest;
Rememb'ring his heroic life — he always gave his best —
That "FAITHFUL UNTO DEATH" he was — this tribute I would bring,
And lay a laurel chaplet on the grave of JABEZ KING.

(*Times*, 21 September 1918)

Dowler's summer "camp" was in Oak Bay, a favorite spot for holiday-makers c. 1900. The poem contains the first hint (in this book) of the European catastrophe which would help fundamentally to change Victoria.

---

* Dowler's only son, aged twenty-five, was killed at Vimy Ridge in 1917.

GOLD!

Victoria's relative isolation from the wider world — especially the United States — was briefly shattered when gold was discovered on the Fraser River in 1858. This gold rush and the one later in the Cariboo region transformed Victoria from a quiet village to a bustling boom town. The following idealized picture of the miners' lives was presented by one anonymous poet:

Cariboo Miner's Song

Fill, boys Fill! Let's drink once more together
Before we part to meet, perchance no more!
We've tracks to beat through cold and stormy weather.
We've dangers to brave ere we find the golden ore;
Yet, fear not, fatigue shall ne'er make us cower
Though death be before we'll dare its weapons, too.—
For well we know that gold acquires power,
And Hope guides us on to golden Cariboo.
Then, drink, boys, drink! Ere we begin our labors,
And though we're merry, in Heaven be our trust,
And come what may, we'll never wrong our neighbours—
Our maxim shall be, "Brave, generous and just".

Fill, boys, fill! And let us quaff another
To those brave hearts who gave those hills a name;
May they never need the help of a brother,

May God give them health, wealth, wisdom and fame.
Yet one drink more to those we love so dearly,
And to ourselves, the hearty mining band
And long may we live and meet together yearly,
To sing of this new, this rich, well-governed land.

Then, drink, boys, drink! Ere we begin our labors,
And though we're merry, in Heaven be our trust,
And come what may, we'll never wrong our neighbours—
Our maxim shall be,"Brave, generous and just".

("Victoria, V.I., March 25th, 1862" in *The British Colonist,* 27 March 1862)

Addressing some of the men whom he met in Victoria during the gold rush, another anonymous bard offered some advice to disappointed or "blue" miners:

An Azure Attempt

Alas! As I view this town so blue,
Faces I find few, whether old or new,
Christian or Jew, or with a Chinese cue,
Or Chinook blanket blue, but wear cerulean hue.
Blue, blue, blue.
How mournfully they rue, some cursing wind that blew,
Some cursing fates that drew them to this town so blue.
Poor melancholic crew!

If from this country new your fortune you would hew,
If happiness you'd sue, with pleasures sweet and true,
That croaking crowd eschew, with their doleful faces blue,
Do thy calling still pursue with the diligence that's due;
Then will calm content ensue, and sorrow fly from you,
For as sunshine drinks the dew, or a gourmand bolts a stew,
So those who duty do, fade all sickly fancies blue,
Then ne'r turn your eyes askew, but believe this saying true;
A fortunate desponding man the world yet never knew.

(*Victoria Gazette,* 7 May 1859)

The above lines could have been written response to situations described by "**J.L.**":

The Miner's Lament

Tho' for years I have been a great lover,
Fate has always been adverse to me,
But I thought all my troubles were over
When I bought up a claim on Lowhee.

But alas! My glad hopes were soon banished,
My bright visions all ended in smoke,

Fig. 10 The Klondyke Gold Rush: families and friends bid farewell to gold-seekers boarding the ISLANDER in Victoria's Inner Harbour. The Yukon inspired both local adventurers and local poets. (*Victoria Daily Times*, 22 November 1897)

When I found my last dollar had vanished,
And myself a poor devil "dead broke."

Yet 'tis all in the fortunes of mining;
For that one loss I'd never complain;
The sun cannot always be shining,
It must and it will sometimes rain.

But when glooming continues the weather —
*When bad luck gives no chance to repair_*
One's heart can't be light as a feather,
It must sink when weighed by despair.

But what nonsense is this I'm writing!
Miner's hearts are as hard as a stone.
They live here for weeks by sheer "skiting"[*]
And a little well managed "Jawbone."[**]

Yet the store-keepers sometimes will nail them,
With a pretty sharp summons, "you bet";
And they, having no friend who will bail them,
Are shaved into "choky" for debt.

As yet I've dodged onwards quite slyly,
Tho' I can't say how long that may be;
But if hauled up afore P. O'Reilly,
I'll give them a draft on Lowhee.

To turn bankrupt I think is the best thing,
And of the Act all the benefit take,
Then in true peace of mind I'd be resting,
While they're welcome to all they can make,

---

* loafing

** credit [footnotes in the original]

Tho' my debts are not very extensive,
My wants are devilish small,
My "fixings" were never expensive, . . .
I've a frying-pan, kettle, and mug;
I've some flour, though tomorrow I'll bake it;
A blanket, old clothes, and a rug;

That stock I've been four years collecting,
So my progress, you see, has been slow;
If you think them worth while your inspecting
And will buy them, I'll "give you a show",

On Elijah the prophet I ponder,
And how he was fed by the crows;
And when forth from my cabin I wander
I watch keenly each crow as he goes,
But the crows here ain't nearly so plucky
As they were in the queer days of old;
And I think old Elijah was lucky —
He never went mining for gold.

(*Colonist*, 8 November, 1864.)

Lowhee Creek is in the Cariboo region. "Choky" was contemporary slang for jail. Peter O'Reilly (1827-1905) was the first Colonial Gold Commissioner and Magistrate who lived in Point Ellice House on Pleasant Street in Victoria. He was probably familiar with many men described by "J.L."

The Klondike gold rush of the 1890s caused another outburst of verse. **"B.C.N."** wrote a realistic bit of advice:

An Answer

I jest now heard ye askin', in a voice that's kinder
raspin',
For the meanin' of the fuss that's in this part.
Ye must have been asleepin', or with envy ye'd be
weepin',
For they're takin' out the gold dust by the cart
From Clondyke.

I'd like to tell ye, stranger, that the trip is full of
danger,
To get there ye will have to rough and pack;
And every other nation and the men in every station
Must bow beneath the wavin' Union Jack
At Clondyke.

Through no park with playin' fountains,
Ye'll have to climb the mountains,
And to rough it in the mornin' sharp on three;
By mosquitoes ye'll get bitten while on a stump ye'r
sittin'
So to git there ain't a picnic as ye see,
To Clondyke.

And our friend with knife and pistol won't they stare

and won't they whistle,
When they see the Mounted Policemen stationed there!
As for shooootin' and for stealin' the pris'ner soon is
squealin'
Atwixt the earth beneath him and the air
In Clondyke.

So if for gold ye hanker, you'd better weigh yer anchor,
But, stranger, first consider well this thing:
If ye wish to 'scape a freezin' and if ye still are breathin'
Ye'd better start out early in the spring
For Clondyke.

(*Time*s, 4 September 1897)

Many of the gold-seekers were from the United States. By the 1890s, Victoria was attracting attention from Americans interested in more than gold.

THE PEOPLE TO THE SOUTH

No Canadian, poet or not, can escape the allure — or threat — of our American neighbor. Relations have not always been cordial, as during the Alaska Boundary Dispute of 1897. However, in this poem which idealizes the common ethnic ancestry of some Canadians and Americans, **Clive Phillips-Wolley**, although an Anglo-imperialist, admired the American empire:

New Year's Greeting

Shake! cries a voice from the mountain;
Shake! Shouts a voice from the mine;
Shake! Let the hands of brothers
Meet over the Boundary line.

Hands that as hands of children
Clasped round one mother's knee,
The old, old love they look back to
The country over the sea.

Hands that as hands of workers
Have twisted the world to their will,
Have caught the Angel of Thunder,
And set him to drive a drill.

The Wealth of the World's in their pocket,
The Trade of the World is theirs.
Their ships can unloose it or lock it,
The Powers may grumble — who cares?

Shake! Let the hand of England
Go out to the hand of the States;
Let the hands which rule the nations
Meet in one grip — as mates.

Why should we stand asunder
We men of one speech, one birth?
Shake! And God only under
Be absolute lords of the earth.

(*Colonist,* 7 February 1897)

Frederick Irving Taylor of Victoria also approved both countries' aggressive imperialism. Inspired by the contemporaneous Anglo-Boer and the Spanish-American Wars, he wrote, praising but also gently admonishing his American cousins:

Here's to the flags that no foe can subdue,
The Stars and Stripes and the Union Jack, too.
May these emblems of Liberty never miscarry.
Let the flags intertwine and the folks intermarry:
For to John and to Samuel fast friendship is vital
While John loves an heiress and Sam loves a title.
May John and his big cousin still emulate

In the business of yachting, and pleasures of State.
"What we have we'll hold", on John's banner is set:
Then Sam spreads his cloth, "What we haven't we'll get."
Why the Lion gave birth to the Eagle's a mystery
That puzzles most Students of Natural History;
Yet, granting they both from the one root have sprung,
Let John hold his havings, and Sam hold his — tongue.

(*Times,* 12 July 1901)

At the same time, many Victorians were aware that certain Americans lusted after British Columbia. From the 1840s through the 1890s, U.S. interests mused about annexation of all or parts of Canada. In 1892, with tongue partly in cheek, the American poet **Charles Henry Phelps** (1853-1933) wrote — and the *Colonist* — published his

Love Song

O Canada, sweet Canada,
Thou maid of the frost,
From Flattery Cape to Sable Cape
With love for thee we're crossed.
We could not love thee less nor more,
We love thee clear to Labrador;
Why should we longer thus be vexed?
Consent, coy one, to be annexed.

O Canada, sweet Canada,
Our heart was always true;
You know we never really cared
For any one but you.
Your veins are of the purest gold
(We've mined them some, the truth be told),
True wheat are you, spite chaff and scorn,
And, oh, your dainty ears (of corn).

O Canada, sweet Canada,
John Bull is much too old
For such a winsome lass as you—
Leave him to fuss and scold;
Tell him a sister you will be.
He loves you not so much as we;
Fair maiden, stand not thus perplexed,
Come, sweet heart, come and be annexed.

(*Colonist,* 7 August 1892)

In the same edition of the *Colonist*, a **"Canuck"** offered a poem entitled

No Thanks

You flatter me, dear Uncle Sam,
With lover's gentle pleading,
And I assure you that I am
Thankful to you exceeding.

I blush with pride to think that you
So big and great and strong and true
Should, like sweet old Cophetua Rex,
Step down and ask me to annex.

I hope you will not fret and pine
Aloud with deep chagrin
When foolish I, perhaps, decline
To be so taken in.
Wise or unwise, which e'er it be,
My mind is fixed unalterably.
Needless my reasons to index;
Suffice to say I'll not annex.

I seek and hope to be a calm
Powerful and single nation,
But I will be your good friend, Sam,
On certain stipulation.
And you may scheme and swear and bluff,
Descend to action mean and rough,
You'll find that I'll pass in my checks
Ere you induce me to annex.

And old John Bull at whom you sneer
Is my old faithful Dad,
And he will pull young Sammie's ear
If Sammie plays the cad.
And so, young man, you'd best beware
You cannot coax or cannot scare

Me into measures so complex —
I never, never will annex.

"John Bull" was Britain; "Sam", the United States. The legendary King Cophetua fell in love with a beggar girl and made her his wife and queen.

The isolation of "paradisal" Victoria was gradually diminishing, although many local citizens' loyalty to the Empire seems to have become even stronger. Meanwhile, Victorians exhibited the aspirations and weaknesses of most other Canadians.

PART FOUR

Fads, Fashions, Fun — and Business

INDOOR AND OUTDOOR PLEASURES

Victoria's climate makes it possible to enjoy outdoor sports for most of the year. The early popularity of golf was satirized by **"S.E.K."**:

The Royal Game of Golf

He wore a coat of scarlet and a little grayish hat,
He had airy trousers rolled up nearly to his knees;
His face and arms were burnished in the sort of
manner that
Distinguished the royal game's unfailing devotees.

Oh, he played with all the vigor that he had at his
command;
His eye was simply beautiful, or so I heard him say;
His driving and his putting were immeasurably grand –
But twenty times he said: "you know I'm not in form
today."
And after it was over, when the man whom he had downe
"Three up and two to play" had stolen sadly from the
scene,
He called a little crowd of his admirers around,
And they stood and talked about it on the final putting
green.

He told them how "he'd lofted from behind a bunker
there,"
How splendidly he drove a No. 2 and No. 4;
He rehearsed to them exactly his performance
everywhere,
And he trembled with excitement as he analyzed the
score.

His "ifs" were as the fishes that are swimming in the
sea,
But for them he would have beaten all the records
ever made;
If the wind had not opposed him he'd "have got the
fifth in three,"
He'd have made the eighth in four; if it had not been
for the shade."
"If that stimie had not "happened", he'd have saved
a stroke at six;
His foot slipped just a little when he drove for no. 7;
A divot turned the ball at 12 and put him in a fix
And the putting green was just a bit uneven at eleven.

I left him as the sun was sinking down behind the hill,
When the fragrant breath of evening lightly swept his
burnished cheeks;
He was going over "ifs" and "mights" and speculating
still
On the way he had been hurt by faulty bulgers,
spoons and cleeks.

Oh, the royal game of golf is all the adjective implies;
There is ecstacy in putting and to drive is princely fun,
But the greatest thing about it is the way of looking wise,
And gravely theorizing when the game itself is done.

(*Colonist,* 10 August 1899)

The first craze for golf occurred between about 1900 and 1930. Early golfers played in farmers' fields but soon Victoria residents wanted a permanent site for an 18-hole course. The Royal Victoria Golf Club was founded in 1893 at Gonzales Point; the Royal Colwood, in 1913.

More sedate leisure could be enjoyed on the five-kilometer-long Gorge ("the Arm"), where outings by canoe or rowboat were popular. **"C.A.M."**'s poem suggests a magical aura to Victoria's inlet as part of "paradise".

Up The Arm

Up the Arm our party gliding
In a shallop staunch and fair,
Seem to catch the joy that glistens
In the water, shore and air.

All the crystal plains about us
Now seem stirred by fairy feet
As the ripples from the zephyrs
Come and go, or jostling meet.
And the solemn pines around us
Whisper from the elfin shore,

Sending back in faint rehearsals
Every paddle of the oar.

And the gem named Deadman's Island,
Like a jewel reflected stands
In Creation's antique setting
Fresh from out the Maker's hands.

And mirrored in the depths beneath us
Stands each cloud and mossy tree
A duplicate by Nature's artist,
Sweetly grand — a mystery.

Peals of merry laughter ringing
Float from out each sunny bay
Sacred to the Thetian goddess,
Full of swimmers all the day.

Now into a chorus bursting,
All our party gladly sing,
And "Auld Lang Syne" floats on the waters,
Making all the welkin ring.
From the echoes of the fairies,
"Queen Titania's chosen land,"
In the pinetop, ever singing,
There unseen their leaders stand.

Picnic nooks and points invite us
Each with a peculiar grace,

With a smile of calm enjoyment
Creeps unknown o'er each face.

Now a faint low murmur
And behold a rain-like mist
Where in "The Gorge" by bursting waters
Every flower and stone is kissed.

See the angler stand intently
In some shaded cove or bay,
Rod in hand and eyes expectant,
Seeking out his trouty prey.

What a joy to trail the fingers
In the waters as we go,
And to watch the circling swallows,
Twitter round us to and fro.

Now, reader, let us drop the curtain,
And when with business cares oppressed,
Take a boat and on the waters
You shall find the longed-for rest.

Victoria, B.C. May 7th, 1880

(*Colonist,* 19 May 1880)

The Gorge saw more lively activity on May 24, Victoria Day, festivities extolled by **"R.":**

The Regatta

"Tis a very fine day, 'tis as balmy as May,
All hands to Victoria have come,
Every friend will be there, and all sorrow
and care
Will be left far behind them at home.
See, the women in fairest array,
And oarsmen their colors display —
Let us join the glad throng, that goes
laughing along.
Let us all go a-boating today.

Chorus:
We'll all go a-boating today.
All nature is smiling and gay,
So we'll join the glad throng that goes
laughing along,
And we'll all go a-boating today.

Farmers turn out in force, there are lawyers
of course,
Doctors, Gov'ment officials galore;
The gallant Brigade of Gunners arrayed,
And the Naval men all to the fore.
Then the bench and the church you will see
Disporting themselves on the sea
And the Bankers en masse, disregarding

their cash,
For everyone's out on the spree.

Everything that will float in the shape of a
boat,
From a punt to a scow will be seen;
No matter how crank, how lean or how lank
For we're all out lo honor our Queen.
And, no matter what boat we are in,
Whether "hard up' or "rolling in tin",
We'll join the glad throng that goes laughing
along,
And we'll all go a-boating today.

The Gorge's a sight, with bunting bedight,
Packed and crammed with a holiday
rout;
How everybody laughs, talks, chatters and
quaffs,
And sings with delight that he's out.
For once more we gladly can say,
Hurrah! For the Queen's birthday;
And we'll join the glad throng that goes
laughing along,
For we'll all go a-boating today.

Hark! Bang goes the gun — the regatta's
begun
What a glorious sight is now seen.

For the oars make a flash and rhythmical splash
As each crew tries their hardest to win.
The clerks of the course shout, "I say,"
"You" — Johnny — keep out of the way".
And the crowds on the shore cheer their friends at the oar,
And hope they may win in the fray.
Betwixt and between the "events" there are seen
Cheery groups at their afternoon tea,
In the sweet-spreading shade of arbutus, in glade,
On the banks of the arm by the Sea,
Half hidden by bough or by tree,
The lass and the lad you will see
Holding converse most sweet — oh!
It's really a treat
To see everyone out on the spree.

(*Colonist,* 24 May 1895. Reprinted 25 May 1899)

Some private celebrations were less sedate. In March 1853, Mary MacAulay, daughter of Donald MacAulay, Bailiff of Craigflower Farm, was married to William MacNeill, son of Captain MacNeill of the HBC. **James Deans**, at the time a labourer on the Farm, long remembered the event.

The Weddin' of Mary MacAulay

On a point of the sea, in the year fifty-three,
Lived a lassie baith tidy and brawly,
Wha was lo'ed unco weel by young Willie MacNeill:
This bonnie lassie was Mary MacAulay.

After courtin' some years, baith in sunshine and tears,
Young Willie his courage did rally,
And on that same day, without further delay,
He proposed to young Mary MacAulay

When she kent his intent she gave her consent,
And her auld folks they quickly did rally.
Without needless delay they appointed the day
For the weddin' of Mary MacAulay.

Their friends far and near to partake of their cheer,
Were invited frae hillside and valley
While us chiels frae Craigflower came the bottoms
but ower
To the weddin' of Mary MacAulay.

In their best Sunday coats, by canoes and by boats,
All hands to the fort soon did rally,
While there Mr. Stains [sic] *took the trouble and pains,*
To make Mrs. MacNiell, bonnie Mary Macaulay.

Thus the piper did play them a march to the bay,
The young couple looked couhie and brawly,
Yes indeed, she looked weel, the young bride of MacNeill
Wha nae longer was Mary MacAulay.

Then homeward ance mair, to the point they repair.
Where the guests were invited to rally.
Soon they all wished her weel, the nice bride of
MacNeill.
The fair daughter of Donald MacAulay.

There was singin' and dancin' and laughin' and
pransin',
While some wi' good whusky grew squally.
There was Gaelic galore and of good things a store,
At the weddin' of Mary MacAulay.

When the sun's early ray cast its tints on the brae,
And the mist still hung low ower the valley
Each started for hame, by the way which they came,
Frae the weddin' of Mary MacAulay.

(*Colonist,* 1 December 1900)
Fresh venison and salmon probably made up the fare. Robert John Staines (1820-1854) was an Anglican clergyman. The "manor" still stands. "Chiels" means young men in Scots. Try reading this poem aloud. These "Scotch weddings" could last for two days and nights, accompanied by dancing of eels, jigs, and polkas, accompanied by the bagpipes.

OF MANNERS AND MORES

The *Times*' editors evidently thought that the following observations by "**Nemo**", the British poet **Henry Gardiner Adams** (1812 –1881), were applicable to some Victoria churchgoers:

St. James' Sunday Morning

The solemn church bell pealing on the ear,
In brazen accents seems to say,
"Come stricken hearts and find your solace here;
Come, sinners, come and pray."

And fast they come arrayed in fashion's pride,
In silks and satins shimmering gorgeously;
To lay the burdens of the week aside
And bow the suppliant knee.

If one could for the moment stand aloof
Impersonal, with power to read the stream
Of thoughts uprising toward that lofty roof
How wondrous strange 'twould seem.

Fair Nellie, hoping she won't get too stout,
Her father scheming to increase his hoard,

While over all the preacher's voice rings out,
"Hear us, good Lord."

While Charlie prays the tailor will give time,
Maud sighs for gowns she knows she can't afford,
And Helen hopes that flirting is no sin;
"Hear us, good Lord."

Some wish for luxuries and some for love;
Some for revenge, some only sigh for rest;
Some fix their souls upon the realms above;
Some laugh and jest.

I often wonder does the preacher know
What lies behind that mask of seriousness
Upturned before him, placid, row on row,
I wonder; does he guess?

Well, I myself have little cause for pride,
For following aimlessly this idle dream,
Instead of listening, rapt and eager –eyed,
Unto the preacher's theme.

The benediction finished, we arise
Let's vow while going to our several dinners,
To try to be, so far as in us lies,
A decent lot of miserable sinners.

(*Times*, 6 June 1887)

Government Street, Victoria, B.C., Looking North.

Fig. 11 Government Street, Looking North c. 1892: Much improved over the earlier days of dust and/or mud, with telephone poles and buildings of brick and stone. The streetcar, however, is oddly unconnected to either horses or an overhead line. (*Williams' Official British Columbia Directory*, Part 1, 1892)

Women's fashion of the mid-nineteenth century was skewered by this anonymous British poet, whose work the *Colonist's* editors found applicable to the fashions of Victoria's ladies:

Crinoline

What is it makes my form so round?
My waist so neat and clean?
If in such graces I abound
'Tis thanks to Crinoline!

But still I must confess, in sooth,
In many a scrape I've been,
There's no denying the sad truth –
'Twas through my Crinoline!

When by my side I wish him stay,
Upon his arm to lean,
He keeps his distance – well he may –
I've so much Crinoline!

What was it hooked upon a post
And let my boots be seen,
When I was on the Jersey coast;
My naughty Crinoline!

By Omnibus I wished to go;
The driver there was seen
To shake his head and cry "No, no!"
'Twas to my Crinoline!

To something beautifully less,
Soon to subside I mean;
To be no longer quizzed, I'll dress
All void of Crinoline!

(*Colonist,* 20 July 1861)

In nineteenth century Victoria, a genteel eroticism was permitted, made more vivid when an anonymous poet coupled it with some miserable weather:

All the world was dark and dripping,
And the skies were drear and dim,
And my soul was chilled within me
And I longed to see the sun,
And the snow was soiled and sodden
And the air was damp and raw,
When I met by dainty darling
In a February thaw.

First I chanced to see an ankle
In a gaiter, trim and neat,
And a silken skirt uplifted
As she crossed the muddy street . . .

(*Victoria Home Journal*, 11 February 1893)

In 1903, the use of tobacco and alcohol almost seemed a healthy pastime:

In Praise of Tobacco

Of all the good things man has found
Scattered upon this planet round
Tobacco surely holds its ground—
A weed delicious;
No other green leaf yields so much

Delight; no flower has fragrance such;
No plant its virtue with a touch
Of something vicious.

A pipeful after breakfast when
I read the morning paper; then
At luncheon one small whiff again—
A tube of tissue,
And, after dinner, a cigar,
An easy chair beside the jar
Wherein the good Havanas are
Too close to miss you.

Life is at best a journey brief,
And Time pursues us like a thief,
But if one cultivates the leaf
There is no hurry.
A friend, it cheers one on the way
And helps to lengthen out the day,
And keeps the hair from turning gray
With care and worry.

Virginia, Turkish, or Perique—
A puff of incense and a streak
Of smoke that almost seems to speak
In sweet aroma!
And may the good Tobacco last
So long as we to life hold fast,

Till Death, the old iconoclast,
Brings his diploma!

(*Colonist,* 5 May 1903)

Other indulgences — such as excessive food and drink — were satirized, as by **Charles L. Armstrong:**

'Twas the Day After Christmas

'Twas the day after Christmas and all through the house
Not a creature was stirring; not even a mouse.
Papa was upstairs with a towel round his head
Uncle Bob's indigestion had kept him in bed.
Mama was done up with the work of the week
And sis's beau's candies had swelled up her cheek.
Her eyes were all red; she'd been crying all night
And morning found poor sis a terrible sight.
Brother Tom was out late — "Merry Christmas", you know—
And his palate was thick; he'd the voice of a crow.
And e'en Baby Bert, who was aged only five,
Had found it is painful on turkey to thrive.
When noon, dragging round, brought the doctor at last.
The Christmas excesses were gaining ground fast.
And, I vow, as he passed, bag in hand, through the door,
He was welcome as Santa had been day before.

(*Colonist,* 28 December 1910)

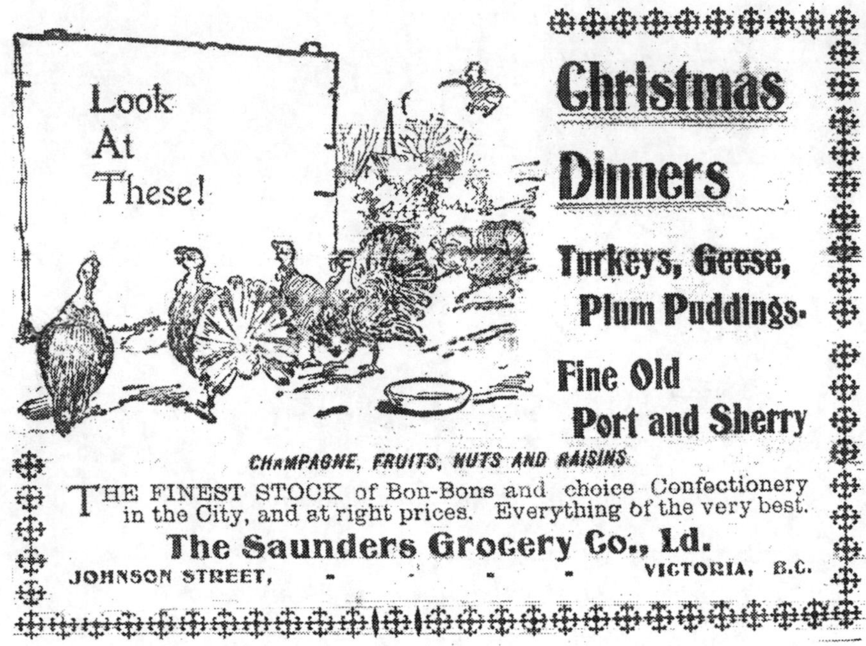

Fig. 12 Saunders Grocery, one of several such establishments, provided most of the materials which, in Charles Armstrong's poem, led to Boxing Day grief. (*Victoria Daily Colonist*, 23 December 1900)

Other fads were more financial. Every Victoria historian notes the remarkable housing boom, c. 1911, when the city expanded into Oak Bay, Fairfield and the Hillside area. Two local publications featured this poem:

Everybody's Doing It

(Some Humorous Lines Penned by an Easterner After His Arrival Home From a Western Trip)

I traveled toward the setting sun to visit friends of yore,
Scattered o'er fair Canada to far Pacific's shore.
I thought to find them doing well at work they knew
the best
At home before they hit the trail and settled in the west.
I soon found out that such ideas were badly out of date,
For all have quit their trades and are selling real estate.

In Winnipeg I met a chum of schoolboy days long by.
He had studied for a lawyer and in his class stood high;
He was clever and progressive, with every chance to rise.
When at last I reached his office this sight met my eyes.
His brief-bag in a corner lay, his law books in the grate.
He'd given up his practice and was selling real estate.

In Regina, next a dentist, an honor man at that,
An expert in toothology, had the science down quite pat.
I knew he'd have the swellest place that ready cash
could buy,
But when I asked to see it, he told me with a sigh
That he'd sold out all his fixtures, false teeth and
rubber plate,
Had thrown away his forceps and was selling real estate.

Away out the prairie, far from the city's noise,
I found a husky farmer I had known when we were boys.
I said, "Here's one who changeth not, he follows still
the plough,"
And asked if he was going out to do his seeding now.

"Not much", replied the farmer, as he leaned against
the gate,
"This farm is subdivided now, and I am selling real estate."

At Saskatoon an editor, a writer sharp and bright,
Who always took his stand upon the side of what was
right,
He controlled the politicians; the grafters, put to rest,
And in the cause of justice was "a proper chucker out".
I thought that in his city he would be one of the strait,
But he's left the adverts and rewrites now and deals
in real estate.

I called upon a clergyman at Vancouver at the coast,
At spreading the gospel he was himself a host.
He was an eloquent speaker; to hear him was a treat,
And never was one of his flock found sleeping in his seat.
His church was always crowded with people, small
and great,
But another has his pulpit now: he's selling real estate.

I went aboard the steamship big that plies along the
strait,
And thought that I had now escaped the talk of real
estate.
On the upper deck the captain was busy as could be,
Adding up some figures on the pad upon his knee.
"Is he laying out the course now?" I said unto the mate.
"Naw! Doping out the profits on a deal in real estate."

At Victoria I met the one I thought to make my wife,
For I had quite decided that I'd settle down for life.
Her cheeks were like the roses; her hair in pretty curls.
She was the handsomest of all that town of pretty girls.
As soon as I had greeted her I sought to know my fate.
She said, "Don't pester me just now, I'm selling real estate."

Alas, I said, "What can I do? My friends have all gone
daft.
They talk of real estate by day, and dream at night of
graft
They make from city lots and townsites great and small.
Unless I, too, got in the game, I saw no chance at all
To mingle with my fellow man at early morn or late,
So I joined the band of boosters and
I'M SELLING REAL ESTATE.

(*The Week*, 14 September, 1912 and *Times,* 1 February 1913)

In 1911 three hundred real estate firms vied for business in Victoria. The boom ended with a crash in 1912.

Even more interesting to Victoria readers (and poets) were the illegal or even immoral antics of their fellow citizens.

SIN AND CRIME, ETC.

The great scandal of 1861 was the elopement of Sir James Douglas' daughter Alice (1844 -1928) with her father's Secretary Charles Good (b. 1830). **Benjamin Pitt Griffin** (1809-1881), proprietor of the Boomerang Inn on Court Alley, described as "one of the best informed and most intellectual men in the province",* recounted the event as an epic saga:

Chief Douglas' Daughter. A Parody of Long Ago

A trawler bound across the Sound cries, "Boatman,
do not tarry!
And eagles three I'll give to thee to row us o'er the
ferry."
"Now where will ye across the flood, this dark and
stormy water?"
"Hush, man, I'm Secretary GOOD, and this the
DOUGLAS' daughter!
Three days ago I asked her hand: the Chieftain bade
me dry up
And should he find us as we stand he'd bung my other
eye up."
Out spake the hardy boatman thus: "Come on, my
buck, I'm ready.
It is not for your eagles bright but for your plucky lady.

* *Colonist,* 5 August 1881.

So though the waves are raging wild, I'll row you to
Port Townsend."

The Chieftain after dinner sat sipping his rum and
water:—
"But where's my Alice? Where's my pet? My
daughter, oh my daughter!"
He to his castle window hied; he gazed out o'er the
trellis
And on a schooner bobbing round espied his
daughter Alice.
"What ho! My gallant DRAKE," he cried, "Quick! To
my house restore her!
Your sire of old explored yon coast; go, catch me you
Explorer!"

"Now, haste, dear, haste!" the lady cried, "Oh Charlie
dear, I'd rather
Get married on the other side than be taken back to
Father!
And by the Rood, my sight is good, yon sternward
schooner stuck in
I'm sure I spy th' adventurous DRAKE! I hope he'll
get a duckin'!"

The night fell dark. The lover's bark by Cupid's aid
befriended,
The land was made, the J.P. paid, and all their troubles
ended.

And in the morn the gallant DRAKE while brailing up
his spanker
Espied the schooner in the Bay quite cosily at anchor.
Quick alongside impetuously he boarded in a passion;
"Come back Alice!" "I shan't," said she, "we're
married Yankee fashion."

"Oh! Is it so?" he cried, "Alas! None Destiny can
master.
Since Jonathan has tied you fast, John Bull must tie
you faster.
Come back! It is your sire's command tho' all our
plans you've blighted.
And as you've been united there, you'll here be reunited."
Back then they came, and in the church both Pa and
Ma consenting,
The pair were wed, all nice things said, but some
were left lamenting.

(*Colonist*, 30 August 1861, reprinted in *The Week*, 2 September 1911)

Romantic shenanigans were also the theme of an unusual set of verses, "Written for The Colonist" by one **"G."**:

The Ballad of the Other Woman

Earth's marriages, in Heaven made
(The bonds unblessed are tied in Hell)
Suggest that seraphs tire of trade

And fling the series out pell-mell,
Results are quaint! Mere men rebel
Or squirm beneath their spouses' thumbs,
But stand secure (where David fell)
— Until the Other Woman comes!

The Youth enamored wins the Maid;
The sexton jerks the marriage bell;
Oh sweetly is the bride arrayed,
And richly rolls the organ-swell!
The honeymoon scarce breaks the spell
(Dear period of sugarplums!)
He's good as little Samuel
— Until the Other Woman comes!

So honestly our plans are laid,
We scarcely catch the funeral knell.
Of bridal passion. Prim and staid,
We half forget the Paphian dell.
Primordial promptings men may quell,
Count him a craven who succumbs,
Temptations righteously repel
— Until the Other Woman comes . . .

(*Colonist*, 25 December 1909, Supplement)

"Paphian dell" is a reference to Paphos, the mythical birthplace of the classical goddess of love.

Other incidents were more public and perhaps more common:

Anonymous

I met a man on Fort Street,
He "touched" me for a dime,
And then I had to stand and hear
Although I hadn't time,
The tragic story of his life.

It made me sad to think
That such a hale and hearty man
Could fall so low through drink.
His tale brought tears until my eyes.
I hearkened for an hour.

And then I gave him all my coin
Such was his story's power.
I watched sadly slink away
And disappear from view.

And then I found he'd "touched" my watch,
My ring and scarf-pin, too.
Boo-hoo—
My ring and scarf-pin, too.

(*Colonist*, 2 April 1911, Supplement)

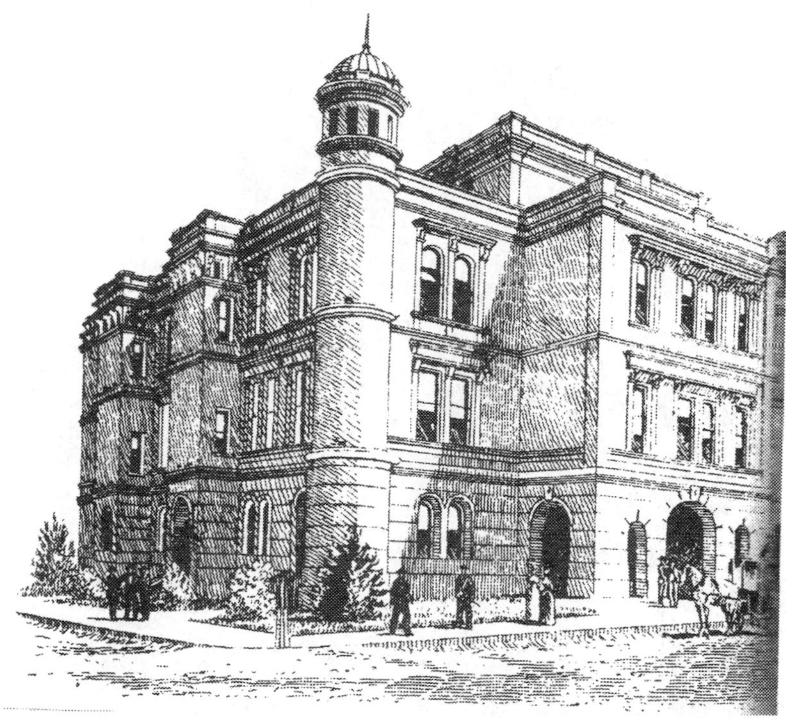

Fig. 13 The New Court House on Langley Street (later Bastion Square): Designed by Otto Tiedemann and finished in 1889, the new law courts building suggested the growing stability and progress of the former gold rush boom town. (Martin Segger and Douglas Franklin, *Victoria. A Primer for Regional History in Architecture* 1843-1929. 1979.)

Some miscreants were apprehended, as an anonymous poet recorded in 1891:

Police Court

George Miller took in
His full share of gin
Yesterday;

And he'll pay
A five dollar bill,
Or else George will,
If he fail,
Go to Jail

Frank A. Wilson his calling missed,
He is a true philanthropist,
If you,
As true,
Accept the story he tells,
He would not sell to Siwash belles,
Whisky.
So he
Goes Free.

The larceny of a heaving line,
A simple piece of twisted twine!
In hope
The rope
Of evidence may prove as sand,
Francis appears upon remand,
The scrape,
He 'scapes.

Mary Brenton, present name,
Keeper of a house of shame –
Quite bad,
So sad –

Charges girls with stealing from her,
Greenbacks, golden coin and "siller".
From Paris
The crowd is
Lawyers' questioning so keen
Makes the witnesses feel mean.
Tomorrow,
In sorrow,
Either plaintiff or defence
Will be put to the expense
Of his bill.
Come it will.

(*Colonist*, 8 November 1891)

And, of course, Victoria's two dailies reported on most such incidents — although they did not see eye-to-eye on many subjects.

NEWSPAPER WARS

Today's *Times/Colonist* was born as a union of two previous dailies which often indulged in poetic rivalry, as shown in this untitled editorial poem in the *Colonist:*

An editor bold has taken to rhymes;
Namely the man who's behind the Times,
And who swears by the gorse and the heather
That by going far a-field he'll be able to show
With an air of bombast as Furioso,
That the anthracite city yclept Nanaimo
Takes of its copies four hundred.
Five gold twenty pieces shall to charity go
If the Times circulation two hundred can show
To exist in the city it stated.
But it never would dream of accepting a bet
Which 'twould lose while 'twas taking
—for well does it know
That the number was wildly o'errated.

(*Colonist*, 18 March 1886)

A poetic fracas developed at the same time over advertising in verse! An "Anonymous" poet — probably a *Times* editor — wrote on 20 March 1886:

Fig. 14 The Colonist Building: Reflector and moulder of conservative opinion in Victoria, the Colonist's editors assiduously promoted local poetry, poets and things British. (Martin Segger and Douglas Franklin, *Victoria. A Primer for Regional History in Architecture 1843-1929*. 1979)

Fig. 15 The Times Building: More "to the left" than the *Colonist*, the *Times* was equally a supporter of things British but less enthusiastic about verse. (*Victoria Daily Times*, 5 October 1894)

The Line

Merchants failing
To display
What they have
From day to day
Cannot very
Well expect
That the people
Will select
From a line of
Goods not shown,
And of course
To them unknown.

If you'd have
The people choose,
Let them read
As public news
In THE TIMES
Of every day
Just the goods
You would display.

The *Colonist* replied:

Well, Shake, Then

Our friend the Times,
In doubtful rhymes,
Expresses its assent
With our established views of
advertising and offers its unwashed
hand in a friendly grasp while at the
same time claiming
That all benefits derived
By various advertisers
Were imparted by that sheet
To its mis-led patronizers.

The nature of such stuff
Reveals the author plainly
By proving him the "muff" that
everybody knows him to be; an opinion
that is only confirmed when he is seen
stating as truth such arrant nonsense,
and thereby placing himself in the position
Of other foolish fellows
Who claim the credit of a tune
Because they "blow the bellows".

(*Colonist,* 11 May, 1886)

Several years later, the more Liberal *Times'* editors teased the *Colonist* for its Conservative (and conservative) views:

To the Victoria C-L-N-ST

Poor Grandmother C., the older she gets,
Becomes crosser, more senile each day.
She nags, and she scolds, she fumes and she frets
In a pitiful, comical way.

She is bitter and crabbed; she's vicious and vexed,
While her memory oft fails as we know,
Till all her old friends are surprised and perplexed
As they marvel what dotage can do.

The diatribe, which every morning we read
When she lashes the learned A.G.,
Is a sad exhibition of spleen, rage and greed
Unbecoming the toothless old C.

She sits in high judgement to parrot-like prate
On the days now long past and forgotten,
And worships the memory of Turner the Great,
Then abuses poor Semlin and Cotton.

She forgets, poor soul, that the people well know
Whom to trust in provincial affairs.
They're proud of the men, of their grit and their go
For they can't be approached by "back stairs."

Poor Granny, our pity, our sympathy keen
We sorrowfully lay in your lap,

We smile at your rancour, your venomous spleen,
For you miss your political pap.

(*Times*, June 21, 1889)

Charles Semlin (1836-1927) was a premier of BC. Francis Lovett Carter-Cotton (1843 –1919) and John Herbert Turner (1834 –1923) were also politicians.

SELLING THINGS

The old newspapers are full of the ancestors of radio and television jingles. Some, such as this 1891 effort, were simple and direct in their appeal:

Come one, come all,
Both great and small,
Try Hagyard's Yellow Oil.
It stops the pains
Of wounds or sprains,
That rest and comfort spoil.

(*Colonist,* 28 November 1891)

Others created little scenarios, such as this one of 1889:

Afternoon Tea

Said Mrs. G. to Mrs. D.
('Twas o'er a cup of fine Rohea);
"Our pretty hostess yonder
Has gained in looks surprisingly;
She seems as well as well can be!
What is the cause, I wonder?"

Said Mrs. D. to Mrs. G.
"She's changed indeed, but then you see,
She put aside objection,
And tried that famous remedy
Which did so much for you and me —
Pierce's Favorite Prescription".

For biliousness, sick headache, indigestion and constipation, there is no remedy equal to Dr. Pierce's Little Pellets.

(*Times,* 16 January 1889)

"Rohea" was a form of tea. We have no idea what was in Dr. Pierce's Pellets.

Then, as now, "beauty products" were aggressively pitched and probably with as little real usefulness:

Three Beautiful Girls

Three maidens — the T's— you all know them, I'm sure,
With their complexions so lovely, so white and so pure;
Their hair dark and silky, and the teeth of these girls
Are so lovely, you' d think they had mouths full of pearls!
They were made thus the fairest of earth's fair creations,
By using the following fine preparations . . .

(Victoria *Gazette,* 28 June 1859 and in many other editions)

The advertisement goes on to recommend "Lafont's West India Soap Root" for "The Teeth Breath and Gums", "Jones' Coral Hair Restorative" and "Jones' Italian Soap".

The foregoing seems to echo modern concerns, but the following appeal may seem unusual, if not actually ill-advised:

Mary ate a little peach,
One day just after dinner.
It was not very ripe and so
The next day she was thinner.

It seems to me that little girl
Was mad as any hatter.
For if she'd used some nice **FRUIT SUGAR**
It would have made her fatter.

(*Colonist*, 14 June 1904)

Other advertised products were probably more healthful, at least according to **A.B. Gray:**

<u>The Triumph of Rolled Oats</u>

The chief trouble in life, beyond any question,
Is the miserable state of indigestion.
To regain failing health, you'll part with any notes,
Save money! And cure, with diet of Rolled Oats.

In selecting the brand you surely will err,
If you take other than that made by Brackman & Ker,
Food fit for a prince, and the best in the land,
Are famous Rolled Oats, of the "National" brand.

Like ripples of music, from fountains and rills,
So sweet are Rolled Oats of the "National" Mills.
To babies they're treasure, to youth they are gain,
They give vigor to age, they make muscle and brain.

The "National" Rolled Oats about which we relate
Are the best in the market, all judges do state,
At Chicago's great fair they took the first prize,
And at Frisco's mid-winter took medal likewise.

And now they're competing for honors in Sweden,
And placing the folk of that country in Eden!
They their rivals outstrip, with a bound and a rush,
For they are simply "immense' when made into
"Musch."

(*Colonist,* 4 July, 1897)

At this time Gray was an agent for the Brackman Ker Milling Company, founded in 1877 and reconstituted in 1881. Its mill operated until 1965 near Victoria's outer wharf. (In the 1870s, Gray, a member of the Columbia lodge of the I.O.O.F., had owned Albion House, a ladies wear emporium.)

The following verses need no comment:

Melrose Nursery Rhyme No. 14

Mary had a little goat,
Its hair was white as milk;
And Mary rubbed it with a brick
To make it look like silk.

It followed her to school, one day
And made the teacher faint,
To see the children paint it green
With Melrose Liquid Paint.

Mary turned it loose that night,
And back to school it ran;
It knew that Melrose Paint was good
And so chewed up the can.

All of which goes to prove that Melrose Liquid Paints are good for EXTERIOR or INTERIOR use.

(*Colonist,* 11 April 1905)

One 1906 advertisement offers an inventory of much of what our great-grandparents needed to maintain a home. Note the lack of “labour-saving devices”:

SHORE'S HARDWARE STORE

The Place to Get

Hardware both for field and household,
At Shore's they get them, so we're told.
Rakes and hoes to do the garden,
At prices every one a bargain.

Tins and pans and big washtubs,
On washdays, where the housewife rubs
The baby's flannels till they're white
Are bought at Shore's at prices right.

All kinds of shovels, spades and picks,
Wee ones, big ones, thin or thick;
Sidney Shore, he keeps them all,
For people wither [sic] *short or tall.*

Forks with which to dig the spuds,
Forks for use to bait the bloods,
Forks and knives to feed the face,
To keep alive the human race.

Woodyatt mowers that work by hand,
By far the finest in the land;
Garden hose and nozzles, too,
To liven things when things look blue.

Shears to prune or cut the grass,
Which can be used by lad or lass.
This is all; we'll say no more.

The rest you'd get off SIDNEY SHORE.

(*Colonist*, 32 March 1906)
This hardware store was at 134 Government Street. Mr. Shore (1850-1907) lived on Esquimalt Road.

Other advertisements expressed what has been called the "Protestant work ethic" — or at least were career-oriented:

Goodman and O'Sullivan
Psalm of Life — Revised

Tell me, boy, if your dear father
  Were to die this very day,
Could you run your parent's business?
  If you couldn't, I would say:
"Better now be up and doing
  With a heart for any fate,
Still achieving, still pursuing,
  Labor, labor, early, late:
Do not idly sit complaining —
  'I'm a nincompoop, a fool.'
Get a good commercial training
  At Victoria's Business School.
Art is long and time is money;
  Seize the moments one by one,

Life is anything but funny,
Call and see O'Sullivan."

Victoria Business College,
45 Government Street, opposite Bank of B.C.

(*Colonist,* 11 November 1891)

If you found life "funny" (and many locals did), you could enjoy many entertainment venues, some of which also used the advertising jingle:

Where Everybody Goes

If you are dull and get the blues
And do not know the place to choose,
Come to the Majestic on Yates Street.
Bring the friends you are apt to meet
And if on pleasure you are bent,
You won't regret the Dime you spent.

(*The Week*, 29 April 1911)

"The Majestic" was a vaudeville theatre which also showed silent movies.

Some advertisers combined their appeal with a poetry contest. The winning poem in a Vancouver Island Coal Company's contest was published in the *Times* on 19 January 1911. **E.J. Osborne** had written:

What Father Says

It is my greatest heart's desire
To sit and puff my seasoned briar
And watch the smoke clouds roll;
And through the gloomy winter days
I long for nightfall and the blaze
Of glowing "V.I." coal.

The poet won a ton of "Old Wellington" Coal, which would have been a welcome aid to warmth in Victoria's homes before the advent of gas, oil or electric heating. His "briar" was his pipe.

Presumably such verses were successful — or at least as successful as twenty-first century TV commercials —because they appeared frequently. But some poets lamented the "commercialization" of poetry. For example, one anonymous writer penned an

Ode to the Gilt-Edged Poetaster*

Oh! Venus, theme of ancient days
Of poet's song and sweetest lays,
How must thou feel when clowns defile
Thy glorious shrine for lucre vile?
Ah, reeking with the breath of swine,
In hackney'd praise for cent or dime,
They prate of the Aegean Sea
To sell black puddings, starch or tea;

---

* A "poetaster" is an untalented poet.

And while to part with yellow butter
They plagiarize from classic gutter . . .

(*Colonist,* 13 June 1879)

Obviously, Victoria's dailies and weeklies fostered poetic expression, offered a podium for the expression of public and editorial opinion, and helped to shape those views, as well as supporting (for a fee) local businesses. They also provided a venue for reactions to technological change and its effect on daily life.

PART FIVE

Technological and Social Change

THE MARCH OF "PROGRESS"

Despite Victoria's relative remoteness from the world's great capitals, the technological discoveries of the late nineteenth and early twentieth centuries made inroads here. As elsewhere in Canada, the city saw an explosion of devices ostensibly designed to make life easier, which in many cases they did, but the *Times* editors thought that the following rhymes reflected somc Victorians' experience:

Song of the Gas Meter

I come from brain of cunning man
And my resources rally
To show how rapidly I can
Conduct a business tally.

By many a secret turn I fret
The lives of all consumers
And for monopoly beget
The very best of humors.

I wind about and though men doubt
My record with their railing
I magnify the score without
A single minute's failing.

I steal my devious way and plot
With speed of swift-winged plovers
If gas is turned low or not
By midnight-lingering lovers.

And if some irate patron's will
Doth my connections sever,
I know my business and still
Go on and on forever.

(*Times*, 4 February 1898)

Street-lighting by gas was introduced in Victoria in 1862. By 1870 it was serving some homes.

Another anonymous versifier complained about yet another modern invention in an:

Ode to an Electric Light

Twinkle, twinkle, little Arc,
Sickly, blue, uncertain spark:
Up above my head you swing,
Ugly, strange, expensive thing.

When across the foggy air
Streams the lightning's purple glare:
Does the traveler in the dark
Bless your radiance, little Arc?

When you fade with modest blush
Scarce more bright than farthing rush,
Would he know which way to go
If you always twinkled so?

Cold, unloving, blinding star,
I've no notion what you are:
How your wondrous "system" works,
Who controls its jumps and jerks.

Yours a luster like the day!
Ghastly green, inconstant ray.
No: when'er they worship you
All the world is black and blue.

Though your light perchance surpass
Homely oil or vulgar gas,
Still (I close with this remark),
I detest you, little Arc!

(*Times* 14 December 1888)

In 1883 electric street lighting was introduced to Victoria but, like electronic mail later, was at first unreliable. And the new telephone could have disastrous social consequences as one young clerk at the Canadian Bank of Commerce of Government Street, **Robert Service** (1874-1958), imagined:

Over the 'Phone

All day on a stool in the city
I crook my spine over a pen.
This work between meals is a pity,
But one's tailor wants pay now and then.
So I long for the blissful hour when
The day's stint is done; I'm alone.
"To the devil with Mammon and Men",
I cry and I rush to the 'phone.

"Hello there, two hundred and seven"
I tremble 'twixt hope and despair,
Perhaps she is out –No, thank heaven
Excuse me, Miss Blank, is that you?
I say, is there anyone near?
By Jove, I've been feeling so blue—
But now . . . Those are kisses, my dear."

"That last dance was awfully jolly;
You looked sweeter than anyone there.
Not going next week! O what folly!
May I get you some roses to wear?
I'm expecting six dances from you, dear,
You promised. O come now, you did,
More kisses. Please just one from you, dear,
Thanks, thanks" –oh great Caesar –that kid!

I close with a bang fierce, laconic,
A word that is naughty, I fear,
As over the wire, shrill, sardonic,
A ripple of laughter I hear.
Oh Heavens! Oh don't I feel small,
To think how I jollied and kissed her;
And it wasn't my Ethel at all
But only her juvenile sister.

(*Colonist*, 8 March 1904)

An anonymous poet expressed his feelings more concisely:

A Telephone Spasm

I do not love thee, Mr. Bell.
The reason I will gladly tell —
Your telephone — you made it well —
I wish the darn thing were in — fragments!

(*The Week,* 13 May 1916)

Alexander Graham Bell's telephones were first installed in Victoria in 1878.

Victoria had trams drawn by horses on tracks since 1883.

Electric streetcars, introduced to the city in 1890, were a great convenience, but not all the time, as one anonymous poet recorded:

Our Crowded Street Cars

"Move up!!" cried the conductor bold, "Oh move ye up front,
Push tighter up together; there is standing room to spare!
Squeeze closer, and still closer, shove and elbow, butt and bunt."
And ever as he shouted would he gather up a fare
"There's little need of leather,
If you only hang together."
If you but pack and huddle you can't bumble if you try,
So push the mass and jam,
Thrust, shoulder, pinch and slam,
And "move you up in front now!" Was the bold conductor's cry.

He drove and wedged and battered till those passengers were jammed
Like herrings in a barrel or like sardines in a can.
Their backs pressed on the window panes and when the car was crammed
He strung them on the footboards, did this bold conductor man.
They gasped and groaned and panted
On the space that they were granted
The space where they were molded till they hadn't room to grunt
And still right through the squeeze
The conductor shouted, "Please –"
A most polite conductor – "Won't you move up there in front?"

No dumb and driven cattle – creatures born with horn and hoof—
Were ever packed together as these citizens were packed,

For when they'd fill the footboard they would clamber to the roof
And there they'd bunch and cluster till the axles nearly cracked,
You might think I was lying
But there's little use denying
It is not at all uncommon, but the certain evening stunt,
And we really ought to blush
As we see that evening rush
And hear the bold conductor shouting, "Move up there in front!"

(*Colonist,* 14 December 1902)

But what if you missed your electric street car? An anonymous bard imagined:

Another Pioneer Gone

He sat on the corner of Fort Street,
And the clock was striking the hour,
When he knew that his dinner was getting cold
And his wife was turning sour;
He'd been waiting for forty-five minutes
For his tram car to come up the track,
For he was too tired and lame to walk,
And too poor to buy a hack.

So he sat and watched the passers-by,
Watched cars go the other way
And was riled by the regularity

Of the ones for across the Bay.
And an hour and half went slowly by
And still he watched wistfully;
And even the town's worst ruffians
Were shocked by his blasphemy.

And the kerb stone grew harder and harder,
Till his eyes took a stony stare,
And his body was racked with aches and pains,
And his soul with a blank despair.
And he felt like a bull-tossed wanderer
Astride of a barbed-wire fence,
Waiting for death, or some other thing,
To come and bear him hence.

The sun went down, the darkness fell;
The passers-by grew few;
But he'd lost the power of reckoning
And wot now how moments flew.
The air grew chill, and the wind arose
And moaned through the hair on his chin,
But he only moved to change his seat
When the stones got worn too thin.

But everything comes to the man who waits,
And at last a tram did come
To this man, who waited and watched and swore
Till he was both blind and dumb;
And he crowded aboard and nestled down

In a corner seat and drew
Up plans to murder the President
And all of his gentle crew.

But alas! For his hopes for vengeance;
For him there was no such treat;
He died of starvation, fatigue and disgust
In the switch at Vancouver Street.
But his murderous thoughts, his untimely end,
And his blood-chilling blasphemy,
If justice be done, will be laid at the door
Of the N.E.T. & L.C.

(*Times*, 17 June 1892; reprinted in the *Times*, 30 November 1902)

The N.E.T. & L.C. was the National Electric Tramway and Lighting Company. In 1890, the "President" was David Higgins (1834-1917), former editor of the *British Colonist.*

Gasoline-powered busses were slowly introduced. **Leonard McLeod Gould** (1878-1928), a regular columnist and editor in *The Week,* was full of praise for them:

At The Street

I sing the song of the bus at night,
(And a wintry night at that)
With every seat in the thing packed tight,
And hardly room for your hat,

With everybody as bright as bright,
And nobody chewing the fat.

Let the rain come down, the north wind blow,
Let the blizzard rage and roar;
The bus will come and the bus will go,
The same as it's done before.
It's never too full of people you know,
But there's always room for more.
You will not find in a life-long quest,
A steadier bus than ours.
Just once in a while it calls for a rest
For a few short broken hours,
To return to the road with the same old zest,
And renovated powers.

They tell a tale of how one day,
In the course of its outward trek,
It came to the place where the street cars play
At a speed they call break-neck,
And the bus was caught in an unfair way,
And might have become a wreck.

But the bold street car has not been made
That could wreck our tough old bus.
It simply declines to be knocked on the head,
And makes no bother or fuss.
It asks for no more and it asks for no less,
Than simply to carry us.

O, and should I live a long, long while,
And long enough to see
The aged bus crawl its last mile
A-carrying you and me,
I'd sure erect a classic pile,
Unto its memory.

(*The Week*, 10 November 1917)

After about 1914, streetcars were supplemented by taxi-sized "jitneys". Privately operated, they were unlicensed. **Thomas L. Hughes**, a barrister's clerk living on Cranmore Road in Oak Bay, wrote:

The Joyful Jitney

I come from haunts of soldier men
I make a sudden sally,
I travel madly over Fort
Down Yates into the valley.

I clatter over stony ways,
In nervous swoops and lurches,
I cover miles of city streets,
Past hospitals and churches.

With many a strain my cranks I fret,
In onward, mad endeavor –

For cars may come and 'buses go,
But jitneys jit for ever.

I toot my horn to clear the way,
I wake the sleepy city;
Saluting every traveler
In language brief and witty.

I pack my patrons snug and warm,
There's always room for others,
I carry brothers, sisters, aunts,
And uncles, fathers, mothers.

I steal by street cars one by one—
It really must be galling,
When "B.C." cars lose passengers
In manner so appalling.

I wind about, and in and out,
I'm really very clever—
For cars may come and 'buses go
But jitneys jit for ever.

I hang a label on my chest
To show you where I'm going—
And when a man-in-blue's in sight,
That's just the time I'm slowing.

I'm out to greet the sun at dawn;
And still when midnight's striking,
I'm on the watch to give a lift
To those who may be hiking.

And though I work so busily,
With industry admired,
I'm never tired while on my run—
I run because I'm tyred.

A humble nickel's all I ask,
To whisk you wheresoever,--
For cars may come and 'buses go
But jitneys jit for ever.

(*Times,* 16 February 1915)

The jitneys were "galling" to the streetcar company whose officials tried to have them banned.

Jitneys, however, were not always convenient, as one anonymous poet reported about the car running to Oak Bay:

The Willows Jitney

(With apologies to the late W.S. Gilbert)

By the streets of the City the little Fords run
To the Willows, jit-willow, the Willows;
You can joy-ride for home when the day's work is done,

En route for the Willows, the Willows;
With a nonchalant driver, six jitters or more,
If you want to keep warm you may sit on the floor.
When you wish to alight you climb over the door,
As you jit to the Willows, the Willows!

Should your bungalow stand in the wilds of Ross Bay,
You must jitney by way of the Willows,
For wherever you live it's a deuce of a way,
If they take you by way of the Willows!
When I asked once for Moss Street, the driver replied,
"Step aboard, Sir, there's room for another inside.
You go round by the beach and then swim with the tide,
From the willowy, billowy Willows."

(*The Victorian*, 24 April 1915)

Despite annoying some authorities, jitneys served parts of Victoria until at least 1945.

The first horseless carriage appeared in Victoria around 1900. By 1904, there were thirty-two licensed cars on the roads of BC. **James Herrick McGregor** (1869-1915), a surveyor (and later a soldier) who lived on Oak Bay Avenue, loved his new automobile:

How We Kept the Speed Law
From Oak Bay to Victoria

I shut off my throttle, and Thomas and B.
I tootled, B. tootled, we tootled all three!

Fig. 16 J. Herrick MacGregor: former president of the Union Club, this prolific poet enlisted in the 50th Gordon Highlanders and was killed in the Great War. (*Victoria Daily Times*, 13 March 1913)

"Good speed!" called the milk wagon, thundering past;
"I will see you next week if you don't go too fast!"
As we turned up the avenue half after eight
And tooled toward town at a strict legal gait.

It was not time for banter, we crawled three abreast
Till the Richmond Hill grade gave our brake legs a rest.
We threw in low gear and I heard B. say "Damn"
As a nurse sauntered by with a kid in a pram.
The maid and the babe looked us over with scorn
But I glared straight ahead, hooting hard with the horn.

At Belcher, a street-car came up from behind
And the driver gave Thomas a piece of his mind
For blocking legitimate traffic — at last
We hove into Rockland and let him go past —
And we envied the conquering clang of his gong
As he spun loose the brake and the Tram shot along.

We breasted the East side of Dumbleton's Dip
With a grumble and sputter and slither and slip,
Till just by Jones' Oak, B. said, "Oh, what's the use?"
So he geared into speed, gave a kick to the juice
And rushed Hochelaga with high honking horn
Like a soul borne aloft by the spirits of morn.

But Thomas and I took it slow — by the hour,
With much waste of gas and hard choking of power
Till, hot and indignant, our Cadillacs topped
The main Rockland summit, half dead but uncapped.

Here we paused for a second to glance at the Bay
And the green panorama below us that lay.

Thomas turned from the view with a tear in his eye —
And a pipe in his mouth — "You must do it or die!
You must do it alone! For my plugs have gone wrong,
And I'll surely bust up if I don't push along!"
So he wheeled with a clatter through Craigdarroch gates,
And hit the high spots as he passed on to Yates.

Then heedless of mockers who jeered as they passed,
I lessened my spark, set the brake at half mast,
Held the clutch with my hoof, and all patiently sat
And cooled off the friction by fanning my hat —
But at Cook Street I met with a mounted Police
Whom I called on for help with a bucket of grease.

Like a man and a brother he galloped to Styles
Who came to my aid, and the last groaning miles
Of Fort Street and Douglas were done at a crawl;
But she never got past the Municipal Hall.
For the long day was gone, and the coming of night
Saw my good steed impounded, for lacking a light.

(*The Week*, 25 May 1912)

Fig. 17 Vancouver Island Roads: Herrick Macgregor's automobile may have been one like this on the cover of a book by Earnest McGaffey (1861-1941), a local poet and journalist. Are the gentlemen admiring or cursing their automobile? (*Victoria Daily Colonist,* 9 April 1911)

Arthur H. Styles operated the Cadillac Garage Co. Ltd. By the evidence of this poem, "street racing" was not only a 21st century phenomenon.

In the 1870s, more and more bicycles were seen on Victoria's streets. "**Cadborensis**" was responding to perceived problems with users of the new devices:

Hints to Beginners on the Bicycle

'Tis fear alone that makes delay,
Or else you'd mount and ride away,
As many a child is seen to do
Without the qualms that trouble you.

At first your bike is full of life
And with the one wheel constant strife,
The head and front of its offending
To every ugly quarter tending:
But though this front wheel has a mind,
A great one must sit behind.

Remember this and grasp the reins
(No pleasure comes without its pains),
Yet grasp not tight, but gently press,
And make the pressure less and less,
The tyro's hands are often found
So firmly clasped the bars around
That numbed and cramped his fingers grow
After riding a mile or so;

So let your confidence increase,
And ride with either hand apiece;
Thus day by day it easier grows
To doff your hat, or blow your nose,
And when at least no hands are needed,
Remove not both, nor do as he did,
Who rode along the public street
In vaunting of his vulgar feat;
Nor grow too boastful of your art,
A puppy can upset your cart!
More ways there are on earth indeed
Than those of your velocipede,
An upright seat, not bending low,
Into a question asking bow,
But keep an easy, graceful seat,
And look ahead, not at your feet.

Next learn to keep a narrow line
The sidewalk, no, that means a fine,
A track upon your private ground,
With obstacles disposed around,
Through which you learn to pick your way
Is best; this practice every day.
When out at night, you'll notice that
The hills and slopes of day seem flat,
The roughness of the road by day
At night seems partly smoothed away.

One thing avoid, which brings much ill,
And that is riding up a hill.
A little slope's of no account,
But when the slope is great, dismount.
And have a brake which you can trust,
But only use it when you must.

A saddle hard, without a spring,
Believe me, is a joyless thing.
So buy a good one and confess
Your springless one was comfortless.
And never venture out a night
Without a lamp to mark your flight.
For where no law for this provides
The law of common sense decides.
Decisive in your movements grow
Who hesitates is lost, you know.
When dogs rush up, your chances count,
If small, outpace; if large, dismount,
And lastly, though not least, of course,
Bestow great care upon your horse;
Neglect of rag and stint of oil
Your bicycle will surely spoil.
Be mindful of your ancient pride,
And clean it after every ride.

(*Colonist,* 20 September 1899)

As the residents of "paradise" were adapting to modern technology, they found certain changes in gender roles challenging.

THE NEW WOMAN

Around 1900, the "New Woman" dared to bicycle and to play tennis or golf. She wore a duster coat, goggles and cap and went for rides in motor cars. Stiff, layered outfits and corsets were abandoned for looser clothing. Some women even tried rouge and lipstick. These changes were reflected in the economic and political sphere where equal rights for women — especially the franchise — was a major issue. Speakers advocating votes for women travelled about drumming up support for the cause, something which disturbed **"H.E.K."**:

Women's Rights

"Written for the *Colonist*"

Mrs. Smith from Chicago has just been to town
And men in their places she'll surely keep down.
She has proved they're all useless and quite out
of date,
Altho' they're such tyrants, quite sad to relate.
She said all the women were playthings and toys,
Which fact she proclaimed with a great deal of noise.
She said they were slaves, which was not at all right,
And urged them to deeds not exactly polite.
She told them at home to do just what they pleased,
And if one of their husbands was foolishly seized

With a wish to prevent them, she said then and there
"From his head pull, and I'll help you, every solitary
hair."
She told them the "state house" right over the Bay
Was theirs and to march without further delay,
She herself at the head and that when they got there
To try to eject them, why, no man would dare!
But I thought, if rightly I'll leave you to say
That how to eject them I'd hit on a way;
Let but one of those "mere men" get up in the House
And say, "Ladies, excuse me, but there is a mouse!"

(*Colonist,* 11 February 1906)

Such male resistance was inevitable. Some critics invoked the Bible, condemned new fashions and women's new passion for cycling. The *Times* editor thought that this anonymous poem would have resonance in Victoria:

The New Woman

When the Lord softly came
And a rib stole from Adam,
Giving Eden a dam
And the first man a madam,

All beauty had birth
And most that was human
And gladdening to earth

Came the new woman.

New joy filled the land,
Single blessedness doubled;
Then the Lord stayed his hand
And our ribs left untroubled.

But now, with a moan,
Man is asking impassioned,
From what funny bone
Is this New Woman fashioned?

If not from a jaw,
It certainly seems so—
With physics and law
Her eloquence streams so!

With her rights and her tights—
One dare not say breeches—
Her new living and lights,
Her speeches and speeches.

Does the New Woman then
In her singular rabies,
Find nothing in men—
Next to nothing in babies?

Alas, and alack!
O Moses and murther!

I'd see the Old back,
And the New Woman further.

See, sisters, I kneel,
Though I don't often meddle,
And I pay, case the wheel.
O woman, back pedal!

(*Times,* 4 May 1898)

Some writers (male), such as this anonymous one, admitted that women did indeed have certain rights, although he lapsed into condescension:

Woman's Rights

A woman's rights –to be loved as she should be,
Honored and trusted as you are or would be.
A woman's rights –to be part of you truly.
Your hopes and your aims and your purposes duly,
Your outgo and income, your losing and winning,
All but your evil and anger and sinning—
And that she will know by the light of her light,
Which is surely a gift, if it isn't a right.

A woman's rights –to be talked to in tenderness,
Treated with candor and frankness and care;
A comrade, companion, throughout all this dark
wilderness,

Part of your passion as well as your prayer;
Part of your laughter and sunshine and gleaming,
Knowing you, all of you, all that's to know.

A woman's right – to have, means without asking for
Every five cents that she needs in her life;
Her gladness the object of all you are tasking for,
Proud of the comrade you have in your wife;
Proud of her beauty; devotion; and giving her
More than a mere casual mention or less—
A thing to be round when you need something done,
And paid for at times with a bonnet or dress.

(*Colonist,* 22 June 1919)

Despite male resistance, in 1917 women were granted the franchise in British Columbia. In 1918, all female Canadian citizens aged twenty-one and over became eligible to vote in federal elections.

Few poems expressed a justification for women's right to vote, for the publishers of local newspapers and magazines seem to have been defenders of male privilege. (Few of the anti-feminist poets declared their identity!) On the matter of liquor control, however, their opinions were divided.

TEMPERANCE?

Alcohol consumption was an integral part of life c. 1900. Many public houses, saloons and liquor stores served both locals and the seafaring population. Advertisements, in verse or prose, were commonplace:

Pither and Leiser's Establishment

If you're looking for Wines, or Liquors, or Beer,
You can get them much better by buying them here.
We show many Brands, and they're all of the best,
Read over this "ad" and then make the test.

Mumm's Champagne at all the large Banquets today,
They serve this exclusive, at least so they say.
Canadian Red Wheat, you know that is good,
Bottled in bond and matured in wood.

It may be you're looking for Lemp's "Extra Pale",
We're filling all orders, verbal or mail.
Many other good brands you will find in our stock,
And also the pure famous water White Rock.

If cigars you are smoking, while walking with Hannah,
She'll never object to our brands of Havana.

And if any time you are out of your wits
With a raging old headache, try Red Raven Splits.

We keep all of these and some others, too.
Call in and see us, we can surely please you.
If you are in doubt we'll be your advisor
The reliable firm of Pither & Leiser.

(*Colonist,* 14 July 1905)

At the corner of Fort and Wharf Streets, Pither and Leiser did a booming business.

For some, alcoholic inebriation was a source of humour. During his stay at the Oak Bay Hotel at Windsor Avenue and Beach Drive in November 1907, **Rudyard Kipling** (1865-1936) claimed to have overindulged:

A gilded mirror, and a polished bar,
Myriads of glasses strewn ajar,
A kind- faced man all dressed in white,
That's my recollection of last night.

The streets were narrow and far too long,
Sidewalks slippery, policemen strong,
The slamming door, the sea-going hack,
That's my recollection of getting back.

A rickety staircase and hard to climb,
But I rested often, I'd lots of time,

An awkward keyhole and a misplaced chair,
Informed my wife that I was there.

A heated interior and a revolving bed,
A sea-sick man with an awful head,
Cocktails, Scotch and booze galore,
Were all introduced to the cuspidor.

And in the morning came that jug of ice;
Which is necessary to men of vice,
And when it stilled my aching brain,
Did I swear off?---- I got drunk again.

(*Vancouver Daily Province,* 12 December 1945)

Alcoholism created serious problems for some individuals and households. Organizations such as the Women's Christian Temperance Union, the local branch of which was formed in 1882, promoted banning the sale of alcohol. When, in 1898, the *Victoria Daily Times* canvased its readers on the wisdom of holding a plebescite on the prohibition of alcohol. **Frank J. Angel**, a local poet, wrote as

A Voter

Will I vote for prohibition?
On that I'd risk a bet.
For I used to be a drunkard
And remember that fact yet.
I recall how bad I used to be

Only Three Weeks More

Before Prohibition Takes Effect

Have You Seen to Your Supplies?
On October 1 It Will Be Too Late

Included in Our Large Stock We Have the Following Specials

Barclay, Perkins' Ale, 4 dozen quarts. Per case **$9.00**

Younger's Edinburgh Sparkling Ale, (Stone Bottles), 8 dozen pints. Per case.................. **$12.50**

Brandy—"Our Own Bottling," 12 qts. Per case, **$14.00**

Scotch Whisky, "Highland Clan" (Distillers Co., Ltd.) Per case **$14.00**

Smallest Quantity to Consumers—12 Quart Bottles, 24 Pint Bottles, 2 Gallons, Bulk

You have our guarantee that all goods are sold to you exactly as received from the producers, and not tampered with in any way

R. P. Rithet & Co. Ltd.

Phone 926 **1117 Wharf Street**

Country Orders Attended To

Fig. 18 Scottish-born **Rithet** (1844 –1919) was first a gold prospector, an MLA, mayor of Victoria, justice of the peace, mill and steamship owner. (*Victoria Daily Colonist*, 10 September 1917)

And I remember still:
The demons that possess me then,
Who strove my soul to kill.

A drunkard's home is like that place
The scriptures tell about,
Where Satan and his host abide, and
Where they rave and shout,
And congratulate each other on their
Skill in luring men
From all that's good and holy, and
Then devils make of them.

I will tell you how I came to quit
My liquor-drinking ways
If you will promise not to laugh
Or pretend to be amazed—
That I a man with brain befogged
And passions running wild
Should be ashamed because of words
That were spoken by my child.

She was a little maid of two (she
Now is over nine),
And was the only babe we had, her
Mother's pet and mine.
We humored her in everything, and,
Low as I had sunk

Had never raised my hand to her, not
Even when I was drunk.

I always used to kiss her every
Night when I came home,
And one night after drinking hard my
Thoughts began to roam
Somehow I felt ashamed that I, who
Used to be so swell,
Should have become a common drunk and
Only fit for hell.

So when at last I reached the house,
And entering the door
I hurried past "my darling"
Who was playing on the floor,
She must have had some intuition,
For her lips began to curl.
And she cried, "Papa, is you 'fraid
To kiss your little girl?". . .

(*Times,* 17 September 1898)

Whether or not this poem expresses Mr. Angel's own experience, it is typical of the appeal which prohibitionists made to the public. On the other hand, a tot of rum was almost essential for warmth and courage on the western front during the Great War of 1914-18. **"A Man in the Trenches"** wrote to the *Week* from

Somewhere in France

I suppose we're a lot of heathens,
Don't live on the angel plan,
But we're sticking it here in the trenches,
And doing the best we can.

While preachers over in Canada
Who rave about Kingdom Come
Ai'nt pleased with our ability
And are wanting to stop our rum.

Water, they say, would be better
Water: Great Scott! Out here
We're up to our knees in water
Do they think we are standing in beer?

So, it sounds all right from a pulpit
When you sit in a cushioned pew,
But try four days in the trenches
And see how water will do.

They haven't the heart to say "thank you"
For fighting in their behalf.
Perhaps they object to our joking.
Perhaps it's a fault to laugh.

Some these coffee-faced blighters
I think must be German-bred.

It's time they called in a doctor
For it's water they have in the head.

(*The Week*, 23 October 1915)

In the 1917 plebescite on prohibition, most servicemen voted against banning the sale of alcohol.

On occasion, the temperance reformers probably went too far and were skewered in verse, as here by **Robert Service.**

A Scandal

He took the solemn bridal vow,
A year ago today,
To love and cherish her — and now
He beats her — so they say.

They say he drinks, and o'er his glass,
He thrashes her each night;
I wrings my heart, and yet alas!
I know that they are right.

He drinks and beats her with his hand;
Yet bright Love's tapers glow —
Hot lemonade's his limit, and
They play beziquc*, you know.*

(*Colonist*, 13 February 1904)

Bezique was a popular card game, originally French, related to pinochle.

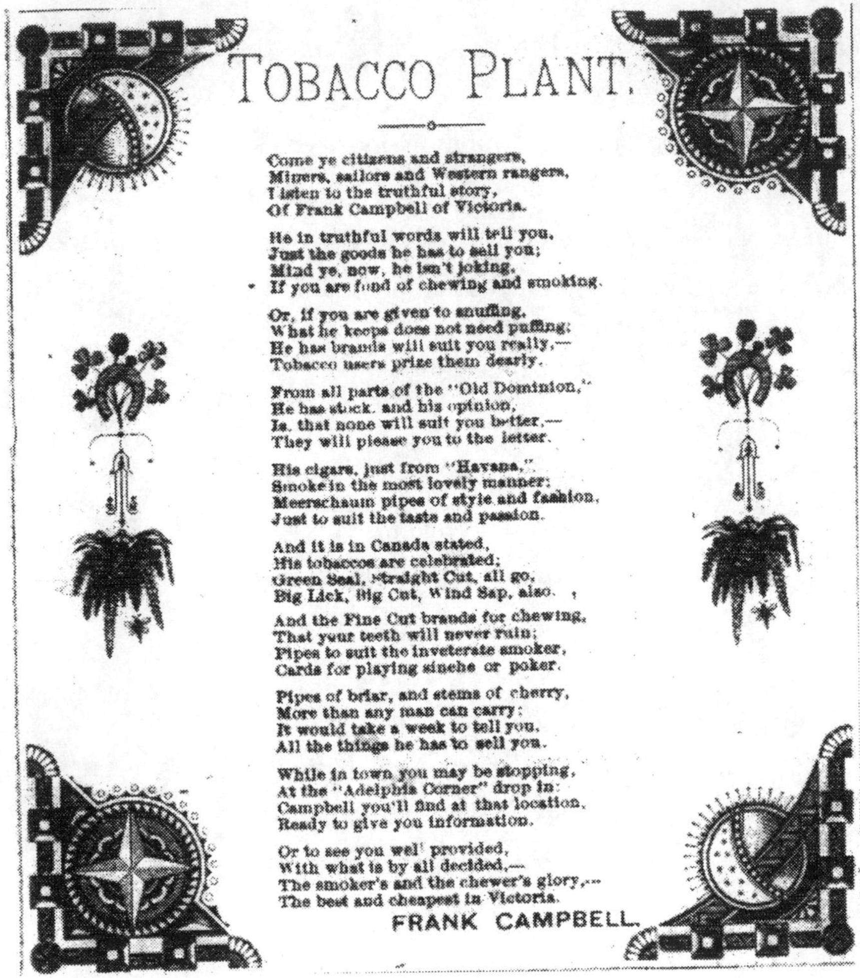

Fig. 19 Frank Campbell's Tobacco Store: The enthusiastic use and promotion of tobacco, like alcohol, was an integral part of life in Victoria in the 19th century — and verse helped to sell it. Campbell's store was at the corner of Yates and Government Streets. (R.T.Williams. *The British Columbia Directory for the Years 1882-1883*)

Twenty-first century criticisms of the "nannie state" are not new. At least one Victoria poet revolted against arbitors who would regulate every pleasure. **William Henry Stokes** (1875-1937), a draughtsman with the provincial government, residing on Croft Street in James Bay, was a regular contributor to *The Week* and a defender of individual freedom of choice:

Our Masters

Once, in the days of our freedom
Before we knelt down to the rod,
We feared not the prate of the parson,
But only our conscience and God.

For then we were proud of our manhood,
We cared not a jot for his curse,
But now we're like cowering children
Who shrink at the steps of their nurse.

We borrow our thoughts from the pulpit;
We haven't a will of our own.
The rule of the Workers is over;
We bow to the rule of the Drone.

Our manhood is dead. It's a carcass
That's preyed on by carrion crows—
Any old parson who chooses
Can yank it around by the nose.

The she-males who rant on the rostrum
The humbugs who pule in the pew,
These are the Lords of the Country.
All that they order we do.

Our lives must be cut to a pattern;
We must not do that or do this;
It's a terrible thing to be dancing,
And oh, what a crime is a kiss!

In fact we are damnable sinners unless
We do just what they say.
We only can work when they let us
And play when they tell us to play!

Ah, well, since we're all of us "Sinners",
We'll never be good till we die,
And it's better to sin in the open,
Than whimper and sin on the sly.

When we were little children,
We did what nursie said.,
And when the hour was 6 p.m.
We had to go to bed.

And now, though we are older,
We find it's just the same.
We've got the same old nursie still—
She's merely changed her name.

When we were little children
We didn't dare to smoke
And nursie says we mustn't now —
And nursie doesn't joke.

For nursie hates tobacco;
Tobacco makes her mad.
Oh, no; we mustn't smoke at all,
Since nursie says it's bad.

When we were little children
We weren't allowed to bet
And nursie says we mustn't now
Or over "tate a wet."

For beer is very sinful,
And whisky's even worse.
We should prefer to die of thirst—
According to our nurse.

When we were little children,
We used to play at games,
But now we mustn't play at all,
Or nursie calls us names.

Unless we play at ping-pong
Or crokinole and such.
Oh, dear, our nursie interferes
A little bit too much.

(*The Week,* 13 and 20 June 1908, p. 2)

This poem was occasioned by the visit of a leading member of the Women's Christian Temperance Union to Victoria. British Columbia held a prohibition referendum in 1917 which a majority of civilians supported, so that it passed into law.

Above all, the temperance advocates were concerned to protect young people from the ravages of alcohol. Restricting the sale of liquor was designed mainly to protect the youth of "paradise." Judging by the poetry published, some of Victoria's youth were articulate, feisty, and not in need of protecting.

THE YOUNG

In Victoria schools, the writing of poetry was taught until at least the 1960s, so it is not surprising that some of the poets in local newspapers were young people. **Joey Gosse,*** described as "8 1/2 years old" reveled in

Winter Sport

I will write you a little rhyme
Of the good winter time,
When the boys and girls go sleighing in the snow.
Jack Frost is then so very bold
He makes our feet and fingers cold,
And all the gloves in all the stores are sold.

We have some ice at Beacon Hill
And I go skating there with Bill,
Until the ice begins to get too thin;
And then we have to hurry back
Or else the ice will surely crack
And then I'm sure that someone would fall in.

---

* B.C.'s Vital Statistics record that one Joseph Gosse was born in 1905 and died in 1970, suggesting that this man was the young "Joey", but I can find no other record of him.

(*Colonist*, 2 February 1913)

Young Joey attended South Park School, where, in July 1917, he was commended for his "regularity and Punctuality" (*Colonist,*

1 July 1917, 13). Another student at South Park, one **"Master Alexander"** earlier had recited

Lines written for the opening of School on January 4th 1904

I've come the day to gie' ye cheer
On this the openin' o' the year;
I ken ye've a' seen Santa Claus
Climbin' down ye're chimney wa's.

Miss Cameron reigns within this ha'
She's tap an' foremost of' us a';
We' Hielan micht an' Hielan grace
She keeps a' bairnies in their place.

Miss Speers is no the ane to stan'
Halvers or nonsense on any han'
An' for Miss Fraser I micht say
She's Scotch enough to ken the way.

But puir McNeill ma poety claims,
He's aye sae thoughtu' o' the weans,
Still, hoo can he against the seven
Expec' reward excep' in Heaven?

I ken Miss Simpson does her best
To teach us mair than a' the rest;
An' aye she grees us wi' a smile
E'en tho" she's thinkind' a' the while.

An' Miss Maclean, she's lo'ed by a';
She need nae strain to teach ava'
It comes sae nat'ral, ane can see
She's quite at hame wi' you an' me.

Then Miss McFarlane, we a' ken,
Is anxious tat the children men';
An' for Miss Wriglesworth we cheer
She's first to teach the wee weans here.

An' noo Iv'e welcome gi'evn to a'
That's sittin' here within this ha';
And hope that nane wil play the fuls
As lang as there is South Park School.

(*Colonist,* 6 January 1904)

It is unclear if young Alexander actually composed these verses himself or merely recited them. At all events, "Miss Cameron" was Agnes Deans Cameron (1863-1912) a popular teacher, journalist and lecturer. At this time she was principal of South Park School and lived not far away on Michigan Street. Elizabeth Speers lived on Cadboro Bay Road. We have already seen an example of the fad for writing Scots dialect. Given the number of "Macs" on the faculty of this school, the poem's style was appropriate! South Park was built 1893-94.

Apparently the acquisition of learning was not appreciated by all young people. A poet, one "**W.V.R**.", living in James Bay, wrote:

A Parody

From the windows of the classrooms,
From the doorways and the hall,
From the little ones and big ones,
From the pupils great and small,
From the basements to the rafters
Comes the never changing cry:
"Let us burn our books and lessons
When the teachers are not by."

From the masters stern and sharp
From the ladies cool and calm,
Come the words which doom the pupils,
And quell the wild alarm;
Which crush forever more
That never changing cry:
"Let us burn our books and lessons
When the teachers are not by".

(Progress [The Week], 25 November 1904)

More balanced was this contribution from an anonymous student at the Collegiate Institute, a predecessor of Victoria High School:

A Medley

R.R. Div. III, Collegiate Institute

A few more weeks till vacation
Then we'll leave this reservation.
No more scolding because we're lazy,
No more books to set us crazy.

No more drumming at the poor old "props".
To Algebra for two months we'll put a stop.
Let the factoring take a rest
While we soar among the blest.

We'll put to use the rules of hygiene
When resting on two oars we lean,
In some cool and shady spot
Far from our old Yates Street lot.

There is Hamblin and Smith's arithmetic,
Enough to make poor scholars sick;
This the first we will toss away,
Nor to think of again till some hot August day.

And a mensuration rule,
Needed only when at school —
We'll use while fishing in a brook
To measure the distance from fish to hook.

The dear deductions of bookkeeping,
We'll con while gracefully sleeping.
To keep books during the summer!
The mere thought of it is a stunner.

Dictation and spelling will be on hand,
When writing to chums in a foreign land.
Composition also will claim first place,
In describing that awfully nice boat race.

English history we will abhor,
Especially the house of Tudor.
Canadian history's not so bad,
But to be rid of it will make us glad.

Some say we'll conjugate "amo"
With someone in accents sweet and low,
But this someone doesn't know
That at this verb we're very slow.

When sitting on some rustic bench,
Where then will be our boasted French?
We'll not even think to say
Vous, parlez vous Français?

Our geography will be easy as play
When we're asked to go for a holiday;
We'll answer in our best Meiklejohn grammar
"A trip o'er the Atlantic to Dunbar".

Of all the studies about land or sea,
There's not one we'd give for botany.
Is it not nice to pick into parts
And find like ourselves flowers have hearts?

Now while we're planning our vacation so
What think you of poor Prof. Pineo?
This teacher all term has been crazed and fretted,
By scholars who are quite like children petted.

It is just as he has often repeated
We should be separately seated,
Our marks in deportment we then could keep
If we had nothing to talk to but an empty seat.

If we don't pass this final "exam",
It won't be his fault, for he has tried to cram
The things we should know into our heads
But something has changed our brains to lead,

Then unto this teacher great praise is due
For he has his own class and Mr. Simpson's too.
Now the fourth division is very naughty,
But the third is naughtier — oftimes haughty.

So if Prof. Pineo has managed us so far,
And has had with us now war,
It terminates in this decision —
He should be given a higher division.

Now Mr. Simpson managed us fine,
But teaching is not in his line.

University School
FOR BOYS VICTORIA, B. C.
Summer Term Commences April 10
At 9:30 a. m.
Fifteen Acres of Playing Fields
In Spacious New Brick Building.
Accommodation for 100 Boarders.
Chemical Laboratory: Organized Cadet Corps: Musketry Instruction: Football and Cricket: Gymnasium and Indoor Rifle Range.
RECENT SUCCESSES AT McGILL AND R.M.C.
WARDEN:
Rev. W. W. Bolton, M.A., Cambridge.
PRINCIPALS:
R. V. Harvey, M.A., Camb., J. C. Barnacle, Esq., Lond. Univ.,
assisted by a Resident Staff of University Men.
For Prospectus Apply the Bursar.

Fig. 20 University School for Boys: From the days of Fort Victoria, education had always been important to Victorian's citizens. A good example is University School, founded 1906, which offered military training as well as the traditional subjects. Principal R.V. Harvey was a poet who died in the Great War. (*Victoria Daily Colonist,* 4 April 1911)

So he's gone east to regain his health,
And we hope with it he will also gain wealth.

(*Times,* 27 June 1895)

It is unlikely that this kind of poem would be published today. (What would the British Columbia Teachers' Federation think of it?) "Poor" Albert J. Pineo (1855-1933 lived on First Street. John Simpson lived on Pandora Avenue.

Even in the early twentieth century, not all young people were fortunate enough to attend high school. The *Colonist's* editor claimed to have received "some lines sent us by a girl employed in a laundry".

Laundry Girls

I'm but a little laundry girl,
'Tis for my like I cry.
Have pity on the laundry girls;
Don't work them till they die.

Just a little holiday—
Only half a day—
Give, oh give this holiday
And we will ever pray.

Our work is hard, the hours long
For us who slave each day,
But Fate has cast us in this groove,
And Fate will have it way.

> "We put this appeal squarely up to the women of Victoria," said the editor, "A correspondent writes us that if people sent out their laundry early in the week, it would be possible to arrange for a half-holiday for the girls. Now good, ladies, what are you going to do about it?" (*Colonist*, 21 May 1916)

At the dawn of the twentieth century, Victoria's citizens experiences changes and problems, some unique to the city, others common to North American cities. But the sense of isolated uniqueness and the loyalty to the Empire remained. The latter attitude was often accompanied by a militarism usually associated with Central European societies but evidently flourishing in this imperial paradise.

PART SIX

The Throb of Britain's War Drums

WE LOVE TO HEAR THE CANNONS ROAR

The image of Victoria as a "paradisal" part of the British Empire contained a contradiction. How long could a remote, comfortably isolated city (even if such a condition ever prevailed) with loyalty to a world-wide empire survive untouched by that empire's foreign and military policies?

This idyll ended in Victoria in 1914 with the outbreak of what became known as the "Great" War. Many Victorians, however, were ready for a major conflict much earlier. Reverence for the British Empire, combined with a naïve regard for military life and a romantic view of modern warfare, made some locals eager to take part in a war in support of Great Britain.

Hints of this enthusiasm were evident during Britain's tensions with Russia in 1885. The anonymous **"Alpha"** wrote in the *Times*:

Oh, Why This Backing?

Ah! Why this backing and yielding
This pausing in doubt on the brink?
There are things far worse than killing,
Cup more bitter than gall to drink.

Oh where is the honor of Britain?
Her might in the hour of strife;
That now, like a startled bittern,

She would steal from the fowler's sight?

The cant of peace-loving hucksters
Has weakened the heart of her sons.
The cunning of Russian tricksters
Has silenced the roar of her guns.

Ah! Where is our boast of vantage,
The renown that our fathers won?
Forgot in this puling cant age,
At the frown of the northern Hun.

Our flag in enfeebled fingers,
Droops in the blight of a foe's disdain
While in many a heart still lingers
A smouldering fire of pain.

We know, and are wroth in knowing,
Were it not for a dotard few,
Who for long years have been sowing
A harvest they are sure to rue.

We long ere this had been pounding
At the Muscovite's granite gate
With our paeons of victory sounding
Over her strongholds desolate.

(*Times*, 24 April 1885)

The gun emplacements at Macaulay and Finlayson Points date from this period.

Victoria and Canada itself were not directly threatened in these crises. But that was irrelevant because the worldwide defence of the British Empire was paramount in many poets' minds — and, of course, in the minds of editors and politicians. In 1896, in reaction to Germany's battleship-building program and the British response, **Clive Phillipps-Wolley** wrote:

The Sea Queen Wakes

She wakes! In the furthest West the murmur has
reached our ears.
She wakes! In the furthest East the Russian listens
and fears.
She wakes! The ravens clamour, the winds cry overhead:
The wandering waves take up the cry, "She wakes,
the Nations dread!"

At least ye have roused the Sea Queen; at last when
the World unites,
She stirs from her scornful silence, and wakes to Her
last of fights.
Alone, with a World against Her, She has turned on
the snarling crew,
No longer the Peaceful Trader, but the Viking North
Seas knew.

She calls, and Her ships of battle— dragons Her seas have bred —
Glide into Plymouth harbor, and gather round Beachy Head.
She wakes! And the clang of arming echoes through all the Earth,
The Ring of warrior's weapons, stern music of soldiers' mirth.

In the world there be many nations, and there gathers round every Throne
The strength of earth-born armies, but the sea is England's own.
As She ruled, She still shall rule it, from Plymouth to Esquimalt
As long as the winds are tameless — as long as the waves are salt.

This may be our Armageddon; seas may purple with blood and flame.
As we go to our rest for ever, leaving the world a name.
What matter? There have been none like us, nor any to tame our pride;
If we fall, we shall fall as they fell, die as our Fathers died.

What better? The seas that bred us shall rock us to rest at last,
If we sink with the Jack still flying, nailed to the Nation's mast.

(*Songs from a Young Man's Land.* Toronto, 1917.)

The reference to "the last of fights" and "Armageddon" was both irresponsible and prophetic, for the later Great War did begin the decline of the British Empire. Phillipps-Wolley's only son was killed in a naval battle in 1914, a blow from which the poet never recovered.

Meanwhile in 1914-1915, Victorians saw the construction of the magnificent castellated and turreted Armouries on Bay Street, with its plaque commemorating local men killed in the Boer War. The building, more grandiose that most other such edifices in Canada, is an apt symbol of Victoria's anticipation of further conflicts.

Before the crisis of 1914, however, the longed-for battles came in 1899 with the outbreak of the South African (or Boer) War. In October 1899, around 10,000 Victorians bade an enthusiastic goodbye to members of the Fifth B.C. Field Battery as they left for the far-away conflict. One of these was probably **"J.G.S.",** or J. Gordon Smith, reporter for the *Times*, living on Amelia Street, who expressed what many believed. His poem is a catalog of values held dear by many citizens of Victoria at the end of the nineteenth century. The imperial loyalty we have met before. The naïve militarism was equally widespread, especially among English immigrants.

Volunteers

The signals flash from sea to sea.
The dogs of war unleashed are free.
Come Volunteers, Volunteers all.
When was the time when Britain's sons

Feared the fight, forsook the guns?
Eager for battle, ready for brawl,
Quick they respond to the call.
Volunteers, Volunteers all.

Who spoke of danger?
Who spoke of death?
Must'a been a woman
Under her breath.
Victoria's lads answer
Quickly to the man,
"Here" and "Here" and "Here Sir"
Volunteers all.

Though all the wide veldt were armed
And rocks spout lead, we're not alarmed.
Volunteers, Volunteers all.
When Britain's war drums' throbs were heard
From land to land round the world
Each man stepped out — the whole world knew
Britain's sons to the flag were true.
The army volunteered — all.

None feared the danger
None feared to die,
Not one among them
Rank low or high;
Each man was ready
When came the call,

"Britain requires you —
Volunteers all."

We don't forget Majuba's fight
When bullets sang to the left and right,
'Mongst Volunteers, Volunteers all,
And we love to hear the cannons roar
To seek the laagers of the Boer
Through nations scowl grimly as we go
There's a Power behind us as they know—
Some legions at our call.

Volunteers all
Men of the land,
Sons of the Widow
On to the Rand,
Follow the colors,
On through Laing's Nek,
On the Boer Trek,
Volunteers all.

Odds we will face on the Boer Trek
We ken it, but at duty's beck,
We're Volunteers, Volunteers all.
We've come and we'll die at the call
To uphold the flag or to fall
To fight for the rights of the Sons,
For the right of the Race abroad.
We're Saxon Volunteers all.

Who follow the flag
Some to the death,
On with the Empire
To the last breath
On to the struggle,
On to the fight,
Over the Vaal
Volunteers all.

Victoria, B.C. October 17th 1890
(*Times*, 17 October 1899)

The Battle of Majuba Hill (1881) was part of the First South African War, in which the Boers trounced the British. "Laing's Nek" refers to the Boer encampment at Majuba. "The Widow" was Queen-Empress Victoria. Reference to "the Race" is a reminder of the superficial "racial science" of the time. More surprising, perhaps, is the suggestion that God ("the Power") intended the British to rule the world.

When the South African War was being fought, one **Graham Roseman** recited a poem at a patriotic concert in Enderby, BC (in the Okanagan Valley). Notable is its assertion that Victoria's "volunteers" would be fighting for "Freedom, Equality, Safety and Peace". Like the *Times*, the *Colonist* evidently believed such enthusiasm would be appreciated by Victorians:

A Conquering Race

O what is that sound that is heard the world round
A sound as of marching, and cheering and song,

Of the drum's stirring roll, the bugle's shrill call,
And the resolute shouts of an answering throng?

'Tis the gathering of Britons! From near and from far,
From city and hamlet, from mountain and plain,
From west and the north, they are hastening forth
From the east and the south they are speeding the main

To 'fight for the might of the Empire's proud right!
To strike at oppression, injustice and greed!
To give FREEDOM, EQUALITY, SAFETY AND PEACE,
For THIS is the right of the Great British Breed!

And the skulking assassin from his lair 'mid the rocks
Shall be driven in spite of his white flag unfurled,
At the bayonet's thrust he shall bite at the dust
For the manhood of Britain against him is hurled!

An army of heroes has taken the field!
And though many a gallant and loyal heart be stilled,
And many a grave with our brave be filled
And rich British blood like water be spilled.

We shall conquer, for OURS IS A CONQUERING RACE!
And soon o'er Pretoria's fort-girdled town
The grand UNION JACK shall wave in the breeze,
The banner of treason for ever torn down!

(*Colonist*, 22 January 1900)

Five Victoria men died in South Africa. **Dora C. Henderson** of Michigan Street in Victoria eulogized those "Slain at Modder River February 18, 1900". Her sort of naive glorifying of modern warfare would re-emerge later in 1914.

Ere three short months have run their race
Since last October night,
When from each heart there rose a prayer,
"God speed you, heroes, to the fight."

'Twas not without sighs and sadness
For those held by memory dear
That they went from the calm, serener life
To the one that knows no fear.

Those hearts were firm as British steel
When they heard their country's need,
Maundrell, Somers, Scott and Todd,
For that empire dear, to bleed.

In every eye there rests a tear,
In every heart a moan,
As on far Afric's bloody veldt,
They join the great unknown.

Those futures, bright as a beacon light
Reaped at the cannon's roar;
Unflinched they stood, and met cruel fate
At the hands of the angry Boer.

It still may tick, that parting gift,
But not to his stroke of the oar;
As he's gone from the waters of the S.B.A.A.,
To ebb with the tide, that rolls on another shore.

Oh death! Oh cold unfeeling death!
Could not thy dart have spared
Those lives so full and hearts so true,
For future bright prepared?

Why could not "she" with one soft kiss
Have caught his dying sigh?
Why could not "she" with love's sweet calm
Have closed his dying eye?

We'll raise a tomb on Beacon Hill
To cherished memory dear,
Thou the blood of life has shed
And filled a mortal bier;

A flag of glory o'er you wave,
As in your Father's keep;
At peace with earth, in Heaven at rest
In your long, last, heroic sleep.

(*Times,* 2 March 1900)

A sincerely felt poem, but replete with the deluded imagery so common to Victoria poets at the time; i.e. the notion of the "dear

Empire" and the image of the "unflinching" "heroes". The "call" that these men answered was not from Canada but from Britain, "their country". Arthur Maundrell, John Henry Somers, William Ironside Scott and John St. C. Todd were the four men who died in this particular battle. A fifth Victorian, Monson Goridge Blanchard, also died, but later of his wounds. A "tomb" on Beacon Hill was never erected but a plaque commemorates these men in the entrance to the Victoria Armouries. S.B.A.A. was a local athletic club.

A more sober approach was taken by **Robert Service** (at this time living in Cowichan):

The March of the Dead

The cruel war was over — O the triumph was so sweet!
We watched the troops returning through our tears,
There was triumph, triumph, triumph down the scarlet glittering street,
And you scarce could see the house-tops for the flags that flew between.
The bells were pealing madly to the sky:
And everyone was shouting for the Soldiers of the Queen,
And the glory of an age was passing by.

And then there came a shadow, swift and sudden, dark and drear;
The bells were silent, not an echo stirred.
The flags were drooping sullenly, the men forgot to cheer;

We waited, and we never spoke a word.
The sky grew darker, darker till from out the gloomy rack,
There came a voice that checked the heart with dread:
"Tear down, tear down your bunting now and hang
up sable black—
They are coming — It's the Army of the Dead."

They were coming, they were coming, gaunt and
ghastly, sad and slow;
They were coming, all the crimson wrecks of pride,
With faces seared, and cheeks red smeared, and
haunting eyes of woe,
And clotted holes the khaki couldn't hide.
O, the clammy brow of anguish! The livid foam-flecked
lips!
The reeling ranks of ruin swept along!
The limb that failed, the hand that failed, the bloody
finger tips!
And O the dreary rhythm of their song!

"Oh, they left us on the veldtside, but we felt we
couldn't stop
On this our England's crowning festal day.
We're the men of Magersfontein, we're the men of
Spion Kop, Colenzo — We're the men who had to
pay.
We're the men who paid the blood-price, Shall the
Grave be all our gain?
You owe us. Long and heavy is the score.

Then cheer us for our glory now, and cheer us for our
pain,
And cheer us as ye never cheered before."

The folks were white and stricken, and each tongue
seemed weighed with lead;
Each heart was clutched in hollow hand of ice;
And every eye was staring at the horror of the dead;
The pity of the men who paid the price.
They were come, were come to mock us in the first
flush of our peace;
Through withering lips their teeth were all agleam;
They were coming in their thousands, O would they
never cease!
I closed my eyes, and then — it was a dream.

There was triumph, triumph, triumph, down the
scarlet-gleaming street;
The town was mad, a man was like a boy.
A thousand flags were flaming where the sky and city
meet.
A thousand bells were thundering the joy.
There was music, mirth and sunshine, but some eyes
shone with regret:
And while we stun with cheers our homing braves,
O God, in Thy great mercy, let us nevermore forget
The graves they left behind, the bitter graves.

(*Colonist*, 6 July 1900)

Even before 1914, **James Herrick MacGregor** had predicted what would become a problem:

Wanted — A Job

We are solid men of standing, in the city by the sea,
Where we emulate the sluggard-coaching ant;
The daily song of Hard Luck draws our keenest
sympathy
And we'd like to help the singer — but we can't.
For the whirling wheels of wealth have knocked us
dizzy,
And of other things we haven't time to think;
We are sorry for the soldiers — but we're busy,
So we'll compromise by standing them a drink.

(James Herrick McGregor, *The Wisdom of Waloopi*. Letchworth, Herts.: Garden City, 1913.)

A THREAT TO PARADISE?

As many Victorians' eager support for the South African War showed, by 1900 the city's relative isolation from world events was ending. At the same time, their perception of Victoria as a British imperial paradise was challenged by the very implications of that identity. If closely linked to Great Britain, no place on earth, however remote from Europe, could escape being drawn into the Empire's problems.

Now, unlike in the 1850s, 60s, and 70s, a long ocean journey was no longer needed to reach the Inner Harbour. The Canadian Pacific Railway had been completed to the coast in 1886; the Panama Canal would open in 1913. The steamship and the telegraph also shrank the distance between British Columbia's capital and Europe and Asia. News as well as people arrived in Victoria quickly.

Because Canada had no independent foreign policy, when Britain declared war on Germany in August 1914, the Dominion was automatically involved. Many Victorians welcomed the conflict, believing it would be a short, victorious episode which would end the German threat to Britain's right to "rule the seas". Of course, the Empire's triumph was a pyrrhic one and, in Victoria, the conflict — protracted and bloody —would help to end the city's "paradisal" innocence.

Fig. 21 Jolly Soldiers: This local recruiting appeal suggests that Victoria's soldiers were a happy lot and certainly their happiness reflects Victoria's enthusiasm for war in 1914 but some of their published poetry suggests a more critical attitude to military service in the Great War. (*Victoria Daily Times*, 29 October 1917)

It seemed clear to many Victorians such as "**W.P.M.**" that Canada must support Britain.

Say the Word

Britain has a painful task, in honor bound to do,
And when her honor is at stake, she fights and sees it
through.
Each British possession hears and answers Britain's call,
Knowing, as sons to a mother, they owe their very all.

As Canada owes the Motherland help in time of need,
Each Province has its share to pay in money, men
and deed;
Each city, town and parish owes that province, too,
In comparison to the size, all the good that it can do.

Breathes there a man with soul so dead in Victoria,
Who can offer no manly excuse for not enlisting today?
Who denies this fair city the honor that we crave,
And hides away in darkness in terror of the grave.

Come, ye men of honor: come ye men of fame:
Join your city regiment and banish fear and shame.
Your King and country need you. Can you hear the call?
Then come — don't tarry — say the word — that's all.

(*Colonist*, 27 November 1915)

Robert Valentine Harvey (1872-1915) was a principal of University School, where he lived. He helped to form the 88th Victoria Fusiliers and later died of wounds in a prisoner of war camp in Germany:

Marching Song

(at Valcartier Camp, Québec)

We're going to the front, boys, to the bloody fields of war,
The fields where fought our fathers in the grand old
days of yore;

We'll fight as once our fathers did at Crecy and Poitiers,
The Eighty-Eighth, the Eighty-Eighth Victoria Fusiliers.

Where once we fought the Frenchmen, like brothers now we stand
To drive the hated Prussians from out the smiling land;
We'll help them pull his palace about the Kaiser's ears,
The Eighty-Eighth, the Eighty-Eighth Victoria Fusiliers.

We'll see those gallant regiments whose fame shall never die,
Whose colors tell the story of courage proud and high;
And when we fight beside them, there'll be no doubts or fears,
In the Eighty-Eighth, the Eighty-Eighth Victoria Fusiliers.

Now England pledged her honor to a nation weak and small,
'Twas but a "scrap of paper," but her honor's all in all;
So that is why they send for us, through young we be in years,
The Eighty-Eighth, the Eighty-Eighth Victoria Fusiliers.

And when the war is over, and we see our homes once more
We'll tell again the story of the part we bore in war;
And proudly spread our colors, and give three hearty cheers,

For the Eighty-Eighth, the Eighty-Eighth Victoria
Fusiliers.

(*Colonist*, 16 September 1914, editorial page)

Many civilians — and even recruits — imagined that going into battle would be a glamorous experience with trumpets sounding, banners flapping and bugles blaring. **Earl Simonson** (d. 1925) was an American poet, but the *Times* believed that his poem was worth publishing for its inspiring imagery — and because many Victorians shared in its illusions: :

The Knights Come Riding

It may be but a little thing, you say,
That horsemen charge again in Europe. No,
'Tis not a little thing. The long ago
Shines around it in high splendor and there play
About the deed a shimmering array
Of knightly swords. With solemn tread and slow
The mouldering barons ride from Rhine to Po,
Sweep back to flame athwart our modern day.
Yea, back through the drab rain of shell and shot
The knights come riding, and the purple cup
Is tinged again with silver. Launcelot
Shakes high his fabled blade in the face of Krupp!
The swift sword cuts again the Gordian knot —
Light stirs, and the dead centuries look up.

(*Times*, 23 September 1916)
Krupp was a major German manufacturer of steel products. Launcelot was one of the knights of King Arthur's Round Table. Reference to "the Gordian knot" recalls the tale associated often with Alexander the Great of a seemingly intractable problem which is resolved ingeniously. The poets seem to have believed that cavalry charges would put an end to static trench warfare.

After a year of apparently unending warfare, more soldiers were needed and men were vigorously encouraged to enlist. **Frank Burrell** (1861-1928), office manager with Pemberton and Son Real Estate and secretary of the Anglican synod of BC, living in Oak Bay, urged young men to

Do It Today

Surely you will do your duty
To your Country, King and Mother.
'Tis not fair that you should shirk it.
Act the part of friend and brother
To your pals, who now are fighting.
Think of those who fought and died,
Died for you, so do the right thing.
Join today, swim with the tide.

You are wanted right away,
Play the game for all you're worth;
Time is pressing, don't delay:
Show our pride in British birth.
Don't be forced to do your share.

Willing work is easier far.
Compulsion's horrid, do not dare
To miss the glory, fame, of war.

You do not know what may be our future,
You do know that is needed now —
Men, true men, not German kultur,
So do your best to lay it low.
Just lay to heart, poor Belgium's woe
And France and Russia's sorry plight:
Enlist to slay so vile a foe;
Say now, right now, I'll fight.

(*Colonist*, 8 August 1915, editorial page)

The appeal to "play the game" (to "do one's duty") would have found a response in Victoria's educated and patriotic circles because the English poet Henry Newbolt (1862-1938) had popularized the phrase in his poem "Vitai Lampada" of 1892.

The reality of modern mechanized battle undercut the illusions of many soldiers, including Captain **Kenneth George Halley** (1880-1955) of Ganges, Saltspring Island, who described scenes neither romantic nor heroic:

Afterwards

The battle's over now, the regiments stand
Shattered and worn upon the ridge they've won,
Staring with weary eyes o'er "No Man's Land,"

Clouded in smoke which masks the morning sun
Praying a quick relief may come before
Endurance dies, and they can fight no more.

A silence settles down o'er the battle ground,
The brazen voices of the guns are still,
Tho' every breach contains a waiting round
Eager to scream cross the captured hill,
To headlong hurl the hostile legions back
And crumble to the dust their fierce attack.

The battle's over now, the joy bells peal,
And all thro' Britain's Empire hand clasps hand;
The platform speakers praise our wall of steel;
Hysteric crowds cheer madly thro' the land.
But could they see the ground that we have won,
They'd cease their cheering e'er they well begun.

Blackened and scarred, scorched by a poisoned breath,
Stand remnants of a forest dead and still;
Nothing could live before the hand of death
Which fell with dread precision on the hill.
And other forms in gray and khaki dressed
Lie 'neath the trees in never-ending rest.

Crater joins crater where the great shells came,
Amid the tangled wire and liquid mud,
Where ruined villages still smoke and flame,

And streamlets turn to pools of slime and blood.
While here and there its day of warfare done,
Half hid in earth there lies a shattered gun.

Look near the forts that drown the captured hill,
Mixed with the clay and trampled in the mire,
Small grim-faced heaps are lying stiff and still,
Caught by the blast of dread machine gun fire;
They fell a ripened harvest to the gun
And every man is some poor mother's son.

But watch the ridge: a sudden movement there;
A hushed expectancy that one can feel
As tho' some mighty voice had cried "Beware!"
See from the hostile trench a gleam of steel,
Then high above a brilliant rocket soars,
And down between the lines the barrage roars.

Gone is the silence — nerve destroying screams
Herald the shells which hurtle thro' the air;
Columns of mud spout up in fan-shaped streams,
Splinters of steel are shrieking everywhere,
While powder smoke, a reeking, dusky pall,
Falls like a great drop curtain over all.

Thro' the dense fog the rifle bullets whine;
Rattling machine guns hurl their leaden rain:
Wave after wave breaks on the thinning line,

Rolling away to form and charge again,
While thro' this hellish music loudly runs
The never ending thunder of the guns.

Crowded and close the wavering advance
Crouches to burst of shrapnel overhead.
Down thro' their ranks the high explosives dance,
Hell's imps and outcasts dancing for the dead.
All wreathed in smoke that ghoulish ballet there,
Mocks these poor wrecks who lie too still to care.

Grumbling and slow the thunder dies away
Like some gorged beast by slaughter satisfied.
Slowly the smoke lifts and the light of day
Floods to the ridge where countless men have died.
Look you of England, see them lying there,
Stout, stalwart sons your Empire ill could spare.

See once that sight, and conscience bids you pause.
Think for yourself and never mind your cheers;
What can you do to aid your country's cause;
How can you help to dry your Empire's tears.
So give your all, for nothing less will do;
Think of those dead who gave their all for you.

(*Colonist,* 13 March 1918)

Halley's mixture of realism and idealism probably reflected the attitudes of most Victoria soldiers who had no choice but to "carry on". Their war had long ceased to be a glorious adventure and even occasionally seemed absurd.

OUR "BOYS" AT WAR

Victoria's volunteers enlisted with high hopes of a great adventure in a noble cause but, even before going overseas, some were disillusioned by the mundane realities of soldiering. In "Making a Soldier", the anonymous poet described what he claimed were his experiences "at a western school" (the Willows camp), where "you walk, and stand, and eat by rule." The six exasperated verses were published in the *Times*, on 4 September 1914. Part of the poem described a subaltern's response to drill:

So he held his head, as they say in the book
As if he was having his picture took.
Then he closed his heels and clamped his knees
And slapped his hands, at the stand at ease,
He twisted his neck in a soldier's kink
He fixed his eyes, and ceased to wink.
But his weary brain did nothing but think
What the h--- is the use of all this?

The second verse ended,

The sergeant instructor, so bronzed and grey,
With his pacing stick followed him night and day,
But beneath his breath God heard him say:
"What a d..... old fool the man is." . . .

Once in England, many a recruit found military life no more meaningful. The "Elegy Written in a Country Church-Yard" by Thomas Gray in 1751, a poem which many a youth had to memorize in school, was lampooned by "**R.A.L**". "a Victoria boy" at the time training in Shorncliffe Camp, England". In part it reads,

Now fade the glimmering candles that we buy,
And for a few short hours a stillness holds,
Save where a man with midnight pass reels by,
Or night's made hideous by the men with colds. . . .

Beneath those bell-tents, old, and torn and frayed,
Where reeks the air, and many a strange thing creeps,
Deep in his blankets thick, and bed unmade,
Each weary, dreary, beery soldier sleeps. . . .

Let not headquarters mock their lack of toil,
Their awkward gait, their drill-evading tricks.
Nor M.O.'s hear with a disdainful smile
The weak and lame excuses of the sick.

Nor you, ye Home Guard, think it not a crime
If daily on their boots no shine they raise,
If buttons, tarnish, tunics cake with grime,
When they must sleep in them for days and days.

The boast of ribbons, nor the pomp of spurs,
Nor all the stripes of which a man could think,

Can keep canteens open after hours.
The paths of pleasure lead but to the clink.

(*Colonist*, 23 June 1917)

Once in the trenches, life was even more of a trial, and not only because of German shells and bullets. **Edward M.B. Vaughan** (1887-1917), a much-published local soldier-poet, killed in action, described one aspect of the situation well:

We've plenty of bully beef, biscuits and tea,
We get enough cheese for to block up the sea;
We shave in the marmalade tins by the score;
The sight of a bean tin no more we can bear.
We've bacon for breakfast and butter for tea,
Yet still there's a question arises to me —
To build of the bully a dugout we plan —
But what has become of the Strawberry Jam?

(*Colonist,* 19 July 1917)

Generally, soldier-poets did not write about the real terrors of modern combat — of if they did, their work were not published. Occasionally, however, as in Halley's long poem, the painful realities of their experience surfaced. **Ralph Younghusband,** a soldier from the Duncan area, submitted

Somewhere in France

(In loving and affectionate memory of my dear friend, Lieutenant James Douglas Hodding, who gave his life for his country at the early age of seventeen, at La Boiselle, France, July 10, 1916.)

Somewhere in France, dear comrade, you are lying,
Beneath a wooden cross, which seems to rise
Out of an anguished soil, whose fevered crying
Calls out on God, in pain of sacrifice.

Somewhere in France! My soul goes forth to greet you.
You are not dead! But only sleep, I know.
And on the other side, I hope to meet you,
Dear gallant boy, I loved and cherished so.

(*Times,* 11 August 1918.)
Hodding was also from Duncan, BC.

Expressing what must have been a common attitude to military service, **Charles Armstrong** expressed a fatalism about death, devoid of any sense of "noble sacrifice":

When I kick in —
(God knows how it may come)
There, in the muck of some shell-shattered plain,
After long hours of misery in the rain,
There'll be no tuck and roll of muffled drum
When I kick in.

When I kick in —
Just think the best of me:
Think of the good things I had hoped to do,
Forgetting those I'd done were all too few,
Some part lives on. Just plant the rest of me
When I kick in.

When I kick in—
Just send along a line:
To tell Her and the Boy I needed them—
That all my love my heart conceded them,
And I am waiting where the Great Suns shine,
When I kick in.

(*The Western Scot*, 19 July 1916, and *The Western Scot Commemorative Edition*, 43.)

Censorship of soldiers' letters prevented the worst parts of the trench experience (lice, rats, corpses, fear) from being widely known in Victoria but a partial exception were the works of **Kenneth George Halley** Ganges, such as

The Face at Courcelette:
An incident of the night of September 15, 1916

The circling smoke when the shrapnel broke was an
awe-inspiring sight,
And the shells came in with a deafening din and a
blinding blaze of light;

But of all the sights of those dreadful nights there's
one I can't forget —
It's a fire-swept space, and a soldier's face on the
ridge near Courcelette.

The night was bright with the star shell's light and a
full moon over head,
And it seemed to sigh, as it gazed from high at the
ranks of scattered dead:
But the dead slept sound on the trampled ground, in
their gray or khaki dress,
And for them at least all this hell had ceased, and
they'd earned their endless rest.

But one lay still on the muddy hill, and he seemed to
bid me stay.
So I left the trench on the limestone bench for the
place where the soldier lay,
With his clothes all mud, and his breast all blood, and
his feet in a gun-wheel rut.
With his stiff left hand on his rifle band and his right
on the broken butt.

Then I heard no more of the awful roar, and the
scream of the iron tide
As it swept the place, for I saw this face as I knelt by
the dead man's side.
'Twas the face, I knew, of a man who'd go to the
mouth of a hostile gun,

Of a man who knew what he had to do, and who felt
that his work was done.

Who had done his best and who'd earned his rest,
where the voices of war are still.
For I read that look like an open book, as I knelt on
the shell swept hill;
His bayonet gleamed in the light that streamed as the
brilliant star shells broke.
Then calm and clear to my shell stunned ear it
seemed that the dead voice spoke.

"My day is done and my race is run, and I'm one that
has to pay,
But I'd rather fall at my country's call than be one
who stayed away.
Our work's not done, it has just begun, in spite of the
thousands gone,
So we leave you here, and your duty's clear — It's for
you to 'carry on'."

Then I heard a call from the sand-bagged wall and it
cut thro' my numbing brain,
Till I heard the roar of the guns once more and the
scream of the iron rain.
So I left him there in the star shell's glare, while the
moon frowned overhead,
For my place was then with the living men, and not
with the useless dead.

The days fly fast and a long time's past since I
climbed from the blown-in trench
And knelt by the side of the man who died on the
muddy lime-stone bench.
Tho' many nights show their fearful sights, still there's
one I can't forget
It's the moonlit space and the still dead face of the
man at Courcelette.

(*Colonist,* 16 December 1916)
The Battle of Courcelette was part of_the Battle of the Somme.

Although some Victoria soldiers were articulate about their battlefield experience, most local soldiers were mute during the conflict and later. A very few, like **Ralf Sheldon-Williams** (b. 1875) of Cowichan, wrote about how he had been "granted the privilege of taking part" in the war. Of the "Hundred Days", the last Canadian campaign in the war, which helped to drive the Germans to defeat, he wrote

Ah! But it was good to live through
That Century of Dazzling suns, and good
I think it must have been to die.

---

* (*The Canadian Front in France and Flanders,* Toronto: Macmillan, 1920; *A Brief Outline of the Story of the Canadian Grenadier Guards and the First Months of the Royal Montreal Regiment in the Great War*, Montreal: Gazette, 1923.)

THE GERMAN ENEMY

By 1914, Germany's bumbling foreign and military policies had alienated Allied public opinion. Victoria's editors stimulated hatred of Germany by publishing "atrocity stories" and sensational poems such as these lines by **William McColgan** of New Zealand. The *Times*' editors seem to have believed that their message was meaningful to Victoria readers.

The Hun — His Mark

The Hun — his mark — I saw it first
In an open boat at sea,
Where a woman crouched in the frozen shrouds
With a whimpering child on her knee,
And strong men bent to their task at the oars
And their hearts were full of hate
For a man lay dead at the woman's feet,
A man who had been her mate;
And the whimpering child that clawed at her breast
(Dear God, how can such things be done!),
With the bleeding stumps of its tiny arms
Blown off by a German gun.

I saw it next on a woman's throat
As she lay on her pillaged bed—

A fair-haired, blue-eyed winsome lass —
Oh, how can the thing be said!
Her pure young soul was safe with God
But her body had been through Hell;
And the thing that was done in that blood-soaked room
Was the thing that I dare not tell,
But this I know, and make it plain
So that each may understand;
The bloody mark on her fair white throat
Was the print of a German hand.

I saw it last on a dead man's face,
A man who had stayed behind
Safe, as he thought, from the "war god's" toll,
Secure from the "red mill's" grind
But he sickened and died on his own threshold
From a germ in the poisoned air;
And I shuddered with fear as I looked in his face —
FOR THE MARK OF THE HUN WAS THERE.
So, for God's sake HURRY! We haven't the time
To quibble or ask WHY? Or doubt,
Just loan us the price of another shell,
And with God's help, we'll BLOT IT OUT!

(*Times,* 8 November 1918)

M.M. Pollok
THE GERMAN MENACE.
—With Apologies to the German Boar

Fig. 22 The German Menace: Even before the Canadian Expeditionary Force left for Europe, Germans, especially Emperor William II, were caricatured as ugly beasts. (*Victoria Daily Times*, 12 August 1914)

For some Victorians, everything German was tainted. **William H. Stokes** wrote:

<u>Gesang and</u> <u>[sic]</u> **<u>Musik</u>**

Last night I listened as she played and sang
The music of her country, German born.
Her brow was dark with sorrow, sad, forlorn,
She yet sang bravely, tho' the hot tears sprang
Into her eyes then suddenly it seemed
As if the music exquisite was filled

With horror. Souls of dead men, tortured, killed
To satisfy a maniac's passion, screamed
And wailed while the fierce cannon's deep bass roar
Thundered interminably, sullen, vast
Sweeping me onward in the glorious floor of sound.
"Oh God" I cried, "no more, no more!
This music I so loved I loathe at last
The very notes are smeared and wet with blood."

(*The Week,* 15 May, 1915)

Gesang und Musik, means "Song and Music".

Other poets were equally anti-German but in a humorous vein, belittling the German Emperor.

There was a mad Kaiser from Berlin—
Who set the girls knitting and purlin'.
You should see how he runs,
Now we're after his Huns
With both his mustache ends uncurlin'.

(*The Week,* 16 December 1916.)

On the other hand, humour was not the mood of rioters who, in 1915, pillaged several businesses owned by Victorians of German heritage. Their attitude was echoed later by **John Murray*** of Victoria in his 1918 poem, **"The Reckoning",** which showed how

* Several John Murrays lived in Victoria at this time. The prolific poet may have been the one who was manager of the CPR shipyard in 1912, at home at "Tillicum" or "The Gorge".

extreme this hatred of the German enemy could be. The *Times* editors believed his views needed airing.

Who will compensate the stricken nations
For the loss they have sustained
At the hands of those barbarians
Who with blood their land has stained?

Who'll enforce due reparation
For their sufferings and their pain?
Who will make due expiation
For the millions maimed or slain?

Will those monsters most inhuman
Be forced to pay for this their guilt?
Yet what is all that they can offer
For all the human blood they've spilt?

For all the innocents they've slaughtered
With aforethought and by design:
Murders wholesale cruelly ordered;
Who will punish these wanted crimes?

For this offence Earth asks for vengeance
On this murderer, and his barbaric race!
And appeals to Heaven for their extinction
As a blight, a curse, a world menace.

All this slaughter was contemplated
For years before this war began;
And how many would be exterminated
Before the murderers' goal was won?

Remorseless, ruthless human pariahs!
With an ever increasing thirst for lust.
Which naught will satisfy so long as —
There's naught to plunder on this earth's crust.

All the tortures under Heaven
Known to man since the time of Cain
If from now on were imposed upon them,
Would scarcely punish them for their crime.

To make peace now with such a people
Would be to bare the breast to the serpent's fang,
And foolishly hope it had lost its poison,
Or that it surely never would strike again.

When we believe the Sun his course has altered,
When we believe the stars no longer shine,
We can believe the Prussians will refrain from plunder,
And observe the laws, human and divine.

(*Times*, 4 January 1918)
Unfortunately this attitude prevailed long after the war ended and helped to lead to the vengeful Treaty of Versailles in 1919. The "murderer" was a reference to Emperor William II of Germany. (Historians do not consider that a "slaughter" was planned.)

Clearly, not every citizen of Victoria felt this way about the German people, but the *Week*, the *Times* and the *Colonist* occasionally encouraged them to do so. However, Maria Lawson in her regular column for the *Colonist*, “Women’s Realm”*)* offered the following lines (reproduced from *Punch)*, in which the fifth verse sounds a more compassionate note:

Some Thoughts from the Trenches

Old Mother mine sometimes I find
Pauses when fighting’s done
That make me lonesome and inclined
—To think of those I left behind—
And most of all of one.

At home you’re knitting woolly things—
They’re meant for me for choice.
There’s rain outside, the kettle sings;
In sobs and frolics it brings
Whispers that seem a voice.

Cheer up! I’m calling far away;
And wireless you can hear,
Cheer up! You know you’d have me stay
And keep on trying day by day
We’re winning, never fear.

Although to have me back’s your prayer —
I’m willing it should be—

You'd never breath a word or spare
Yourself, and stop me playing fair;
You're braver far than me.

So let your dear face twist a smile
The way it used to do;
And keep on cheery all the while,
Rememb'ring hating's not your style—
Germans have mothers, too.

And when the work is through, and when
I'm coming home to find
The one who sent me out, oh! Then
I'll make you (bless you) laugh again,
Old sweetheart left behind.

(*Colonist,* 9 September 1915)

The poem was part of the newspaper's effort to bolster the spirits of its readers when the war still showed little sign of ending. Other such poems in a similar morale-boosting vein were regularly published at this time. Conceivably, the above verses were not written by an actual soldier in France, but their themes — the sentimental "momism" and the illusion of inevitable victory — could be frequently read in Victoria's newspapers.

When not worrying about the fate of their loved ones overseas, Victoria parents, wives and children had problems of their own

ON THE HOME FRONT

Already a year into the war, civilians' "gung-ho" enthusiasm was in decline. Many grumbled about hoarders and profiteers. Joseph Wesley Flavelle (1858-1939, head of a major pork-packing business during the war, was accused of profiteering in bacon. Responding to this charge and to Flavelle's elevation to the peerage, one anonymous poet reflected on the man's alleged wartime career, reflecting widespread resentment over

Profiteering

Is there a profiteer so dead
Who never to himself has said:
"This is my own, my native land".
I've got my country by the hair
In what they eat and what they wear,
And so I'll bleed this country white.
They're suckers all and they will bite,
I'll help myself while others fight.
I'll own my native land.

The price of living's so complex,
It even Master-minds doth vex,
So soak the Plebeans in the nex
Before they understand,
And when home the boys are come,

I'll wave the flag, and beat the drum
And if they're good I'll give them some
Of this dear fertile land.

I do not care a rusty pin
So long as I can save my skin,
Preserve my well-clad self.
Why should I care, alas, alack,
While shysters shyst and slacker slack,
If I can make more pelf.
Why should I care who pays the price
And gets their heads packed up in ice,
As long as I can smile.

I hardly care who wins the war
As long as I can make some more
Additions to my pile.
I do not care a tinker's cuss
Who goes and cleanses up the muss
And loses all most dear.

I shall be, if riches I get,
Knight, or p'rhaps a baronet,
Cos' I'm a profiteer,
And then when I am gone and dead,
Upon my tombstone shall be said:
"He helped himself while others bled,
For his native land."

(*The Semi-Weekly Tribune*, [Victoria] 16 January 1919)

The first three lines are adapted from a poem by Sir Walter Scott:

Breathes there the man with
soul so dead,
Who never to himself hath said,
'This is my own, my native land!"

Edward Alexander Wallace, who had been a greenhouse manager and lived in Oak Bay, expressed a more balanced but probably unpopular, view, which incidentally reveals the problems of homemakers:

The Patriotic Profiteer

The public cannot see the present price of meat.
They fail to grasp the principle of care in what they
eat;
To save the situation, the simple butcher tried,
He sends the prices skywards, and makes them
economise.

You get three pounds for your dollar where you got
five before.
That's two pounds left for someone who is active in
the war;
This is the patriotic principle which I so much admire.

Ship the savings to the Allies and — send the prices higher.
When the butcher blandly tells you lamb is forty cents a pound,
Don't leave the store in dudgeon and call him "dirty hound",
'Tis the patriotic principle, you can see the reason why,
If you spare the little lambkins there'll be mutton by and bye.

When leg of pork costs forty cents, stew mutton twenty-five,
You eat much less and thus you help keep other folk alive,
Don't whimper that profit of ten cents a pound he makes.
His conscience never pricks him, for he does it for your sakes.

And the shekels to his coffers come in one continuous flow,
Source of consolation to him for he's cursed by high and low;
At your vile insinuations he can well afford to sneer,
For he's earned the honored title, "Patriotic Profiteer"!

(*Times,* 4 August 1917)

Not Everyone Can Fight for the Preservation of the British Empire

All Can Be Loyal and Patriotic

REFERRING to the campaign about to be launched for the securing of funds to relieve the families of the husbands, fathers and sons who have volunteered for active service in the defence of the Empire.

WEILER BROS., LIMITED

beg to state that they will cheerfully aid and assist this good work now, and at all times, and will do everything in their power to facilitate the movement referred to, having in view the relief of those dependent upon our gallant soldiers.

Support the Patriotic Fund
Give! Give! Give!

Fig. 23 The Canadian Patriotic Fund Drive: this private fund-raising organization gave financial and social assistance to soldiers' families. The call to save the British Empire was especially appealing in Victoria, as the published verse reveals. (*Victoria Daily Colonist*, 27 September 1915 and frequently)

Some Victoria people, however, may have had ways and means of getting the kind of food they wanted, as one writer, "**Touchstone**", in the *Colonist* admitted:

<u>To a Perfect Pig</u>

Sweet porker, though in days that knew not war
I held thee far from guiltless of offence
When, hid from sight, thou yet didst all the more
Proclaim thy nearness through another sense.
Forgive me those expressions of disgust

Of which, indeed, I now should blush to tell
And take my lay which finds you, as I trust,
As it leaves me at present, fit and well.

An earnest food-producer thou, indeed,
Whose very hour of life is nobly spent
In an endeavor to fulfil the need
Of hungry folk for further nutriment.
Nor in thy ceaseless task dost thou disdain
The food from which ourselves would turn away;
On less than homely fare 'tis then to gain
In bulk, if not in beauty, day by day.

Food hoarders, heavy feeders — these we call
"Hogs" in our yet imperfect human speech.
That is the most unkindest cut of all
Seeing the lesson that thy life doth teach.
And, since we talk of cuts, in that glad time
When I shall meet thee at my rationed board
May that one justify the prefix "prime"
Which my food-lottery's coupons shall afford!

(*Colonist*, 10 March 1918)

Typical of the appeal to Victorians to "stick it" and support the war effort with monetary donations was this poem published on 1 December 1915 by **Charles Armstrong:**

<u>It's Up to You</u>

(The great canvass for funds for the wives and dependents of Victorians at the Front will begin today [1 December 1915] .)

Victoria's proud of her heroes;
Her soldiers have all made good.
Hughes wires for some more and they'll go by the score
Why, we'd all go along if we could.
But some of us aren't just the ticket
To be bayoneting Huns in a ditch,
And rheumatics or gout count a
Bunch of it's out [sic] *or* [illegible]
Of the fellows who can help "Kitch".

But that doesn't mean, by a jugful,
That there's nothing at all we can do.
We can each do his bit: it's a case of "remit";
And this, gentle reader, means YOU.
We can each bear a good silver rifle,
With a by'net that's pointed with gold.
'Tis a good bit of work that nobody can shirk,
For it takes in the young and the old.

Out there where the shrapnel is bursting,
There's many a man from this town
Who will fearlessly die, feeling sure you and I
Will keep back the wolf from his own.

He's given up home, wife and kiddies.
He's manfully doing his bit;
But his pay isn't big, and so we'll have to dig.
Now are you going to show white, or quit?

There's no use in squirming and dodging;
Here' something that's right up to you.
You can't pack a gun, now are you going to run
From the only small thing you the can do?
The boys don't want charity, mind you.
They look upon this as their right.
So come on, get the range, and let go with your change,
And help out the men who can fight.

Sam Hughes (1853 –1921) was Canadian Minster of Militia and Defence during the war. "Kitch" was Horatio Herbert Kitchener, (1850 – 1916) British Secretary of State for War.

As if rising living costs, worrying about loved ones overseas and reading casualty lists in the local newspapers were not enough to try civilians' spirits, disease struck the home front. The Spanish influenza epidemic was a domestic disaster which killed 30,000-50,000 Canadians, almost as many men who died in the war. Mrs. **A. Wilson** of Victoria West wrote these lines which may seem to trivialize the catastrophe but which illustrate some of the suffering and related consequences of the crisis:

Oh, the grippe, this terrible grippe,
Thro' country and town it is taking a trip;
Bringing to all a most fearful attack

Of biliousness, headache and pains in the back.
Its victims are many, its ravages grave;
Its "grip" is like iron, we lie and we rave,
Groaning and moaning with exquisite pain,
And praying we never may have it again.

Where does it come from, this wonderful grip,
So powerful that no one can give it the slip?
It comes and it brings with it doses of chills
And then you must take for it doses of pills.
You shiver and sneeze and your head's like a tap,
For you've got the grip and the grip's got you,
nap;
But it's got a new name, 'tis the "Spanish Flu".

But one thing I've noticed that this "Spanish
Flu":
Is not a respector of persons — have you?
It visits the homes of the humble and great,
And travels at will over country and state.
Brave men fall before it, proud women as well,
And children have also been smitten and fell.
For one who has come, saw and conquered all
through,
We take off our hat to you, "Conquering Flu."

But we don't bid you welcome: Oh you Might Flu.
There's nobody wants you, so kindly skidoo.
At your word of command we have closed every

door
Of theatres, movies and places galore.
You've shut down our meetings and even our
schools,
You've treated us just like a parcel of fools,
And even our churches and Sunday schools, too
You have closed with a bang. Oh, you wonderful
Flu!

Still, altho' you have made us obey every whim,
We rise up in defiance, your chance is now slim.
We'll chase you before us, grim spectre away!
We'll fear you no longer we'll rout you today.
You've stalked through our midst like a fiend
seeking prey,
'Till you quite overpowered our brightest and
gay.
But your day is near over, you've had us, 'tis true
And we are the conquerors, Oh, Great Spanish
Flu.

(*Colonist*, 3 November 1918)

PACIFIST, BOLOIST, SLACKER AND GINK

Across the country, support for the war was limited in Québec, on the prairies, and in the labour movement. Given Victoria's initial militant enthusiasm for war, loyalty to the Empire and anti-German hysteria, some locals easily vilified those who were less than keen about the conflict. The editors of *The Week* prefaced the following verses with the falsehood: "Every Pacifist, whether he knows it or not, is giving aid to the enemy and they are all paid with German Gold. — The Daily Press."

Sendin' the Bill to "Bill"

Millions of dollars are flyin' around
For the men who know how to write
And a jolly fat purse for the bold Pamphleteer,
Who can get the peace suckers to bite.
All kinds of money quite easily made
By writin' the rottenest trash,
Just talk about "peace", or "stoppin' the war"
And the Kaiser will put up the cash.

Peace Talk! Grease talk!
Talk of the slippery Hun!
Tryin' to finish the war so soon,

When we ain't only just 'arf begun!
Pacifist, Boloist, slacker and gink,
Their talk sure will make you feel ill;
An' they always can get all the money they want,
By sendin' their bill in to "Bill".

Everyone knows what rubbish they spout
Spite of their literary skill,
Kickin' at ten million men bein' killed
When there's twenty more million to kill;
Gruntin' because winnin' freedom without . . .
Means losin' that freedom within—
An' all that time fillin' the sides of their pants
With gold that comes straight from Berlin.

Loose Talk! Goose Talk!
Talk of a gibbering fool!
The papers all tell you (an' they ought to know)
That you're working as Germany's tool.
Pacifist, Boloist, slacker and gink.
Their tongues they will never keep still.
It's dollars made easy with this kind of talk
By sendin' the bill in to "Bill".

Talk about tryin' to learn to forgive—
Forget it, its all bally rot!
Bring out the man who dares talk of forgiveness—
An' give him the "wot for" good an' hot!
Germany pays for this kind of stuff

An' you bet that she pays jolly well.
But just how the money comes over the sea
There's only the papers can tell.

Press talk. Guess talk.
Talk that would lay you out flat.
Colonist, Times and the whole Northcilffe Press
It comes through the crown of your hat.
Pacifist, Boloist, conchi and imp,
These are the men you would kill.
An' none of them ever got a red cent
By sendin' their bill into "Bill,"

(*The Week,* 12 January 1918)

"Bill" was Emperor William of Germany. A "Boloist" was a Bolshevik, a Russian Marxist revolutionary. A "conchi" was a conscientious objector. By this date, *The Week* had changed ownership, becoming more conservative in its opinions.

The year 1917 saw Canada more disunited than ever before. With the rising cost of living and rumours about hoarding and profiteering, labour discontent and industrial disputes resulted in strikes. Nurse **Margaret Busby** (1870-1932), living on Fort Street in Victoria, wrote with a play on words:

All civil life is striking
For what they call fair play:
Our soldiers, too, are striking
For a dollar ten a day.

They strike for threatened freedom,
The striking cost, oft life,
And a striking desolation
For children dear and wife.

Our navies great and noble,
Who watch the troubled seas,
For a dollar ten and country,
Forsake all joys that please.

We note the striking difference
Of a striking world today
In the noble strike for country
And thoughtless strikes for pay.

(Editorial page of the *Colonist*, 26 July 1918)

Resistance to conscription was strongest in French Canada. With considerable romanticization of the past several centuries of history, **Clive Phillips-Wolley** reminded the Québecois:

To the French Canadians

Whenever a daring deed was done or a chivalrous
quest achieved,
When the odds against were ten to one and the
laurels bloodiest leaved;
Whenever the fight was fiercest and honour alone not
lost,

Steel to steel in the forefront, your swords and our
own were crost.

Whenever the charge was swiftest, 'twas a laughing
Frenchman led;
Whenever the charge was broke, it broke on our line
of red;
The gayest hearts in battle, the stoutest hearts at sea,
Followed the Leopards of England, or fought for the
Fleur de Lis.

Now this is the law of England, and Hers is the Law
of the West;
The foes who fight us fairly, make the friends we love
the best;
The only peers of our people are such as have dared
and died,
With steady eyes on our bay'net point or cheering lips
at our side.

We have buried our dead together, Wolfe and your
own Montcalm;
We have sung with you songs of battle, we have
taught the seas our psalm,
"Peace and be still," and always we have used our
blended might
To give to the people freedom and to every man his right.

This is no time to bicker. We who have tried your worth
Bid you stand shoulder to shoulder, for the peace of
all God's earth.
We have shared this land in common, you have proved
the Old Land's word,
Now let up keep together, the homes we have won by
the sword.

(*Canadian Poets of the Great* War [ed. John W. Garwin] 1918.)

Distressed by labour strife and resistance to conscription in the difficult year of 1917, **Philip G. Cox** (1879-1941) of Beach Drive in Victoria appealed for national unity**.**

What Will the Answer Be?

The day is coming shortly when the world will want to
know
If Canada will falter or how she'll face the foe.
Will we stand up all together for Empire, Home and
Crown,
Or will we break in chaos and meet him laying down?

The day is coming swiftly when the Motherland will ask—
How fare my brave Canadians in this dreadful,
mighty task?
Full well they've done their duty in the awe-inspiring
fray.

Now comes the crucial moment. Pray God their line won't sway.

The day is coming later, when our children must be told
What part their parent took in guarding what they hold.
Did they sent a noble few to fight, then left them to their fate?
That does not sound like Canada, up to the present date.

Canadians, everyone of us, no matter how we feel,
We have borne some pretty heavy blows, at the hardest did not reel.
Let us bury party politics, each one is bad as each.
Don't throw away our victory just as it comes in reach.

There's victory in UNION, UNITED let us stand,
Don't let sedition-mongers creep through our noble land.
Just keep them in their sheltered nest, let them stay among their own.
We, of the West, will give our best for Empire and for Home.

(*Colonist*, 12 December 1917)

This poet's identification of Victoria with the British Empire — "Empire, Home, and Crown" — was, as we have seen, a common theme in published verse, reflecting deep local attachment to Great Britain. But in this poem the poet also expresses a sense of unease about the survival of that link.

LOOKING BACK — AND AHEAD

After visiting Victoria in 1907, Rudyard Kipling compared the city to the English seaside resorts of Bournemouth and Torquay but with a background of the Himalayas, linking nostalgia for the "Old Country" with British imperial experience in

Fig. 24 Victoria's Future? Instead of fruit and flowers (see Part Two), the cornucopia here spew coins and "Eden" is covered in factories, mills and office towers. But a replica of London's Tower Bridge (never built here) spans the inner harbour and the figure of Victoria touts "the climate". Fortunately, in the 21st century, the city's semi-Mediterranean weather prevails, the pseudo-English patina has declined, and the excessive industrialization has not occurred. (*The Week*, 18 January 1913)

India.[*] In the minds of many locals and visitors alike, these associations were powerful into the 'teens of the twentieth century —then came the great crisis. As we have seen, locals' love for the "Mother Country", their pride in the British Empire, and their unreflective, romantic fascination with warfare helped to determine their enthusiastic participation in World War I. After c. 1914, however, Victoria's citizens could no longer relish their slightly smug isolation in "paradise". The Great War helped to undermine the society and culture which Victoria's elite had known for the previous seventy years. Not the gold rushes of 1858 and later, not the completion of the railway to the West, nor the visits of the Empress liners had such a profound effect on local people. The ambling pace of local affairs ended.

Most important, the sense of living in a special, sheltered idyll of "Britishness" began to decline. In both the *Times* and the *Colonist*, over the years of the war, a decline in references to defending Britain and the British Empire and pride in the British nature of Victoria is noticeable. Whereas in 1914 the imperial theme was ubiquitous, after 1915, the drop in frequency was steep, so that the year 1918 saw very few instances of imperial patriotism in verse. In the *Times*, for example, nine poems on "the call of Britain" appeared in September 1914 alone; four in the same month in 1915; two in 1916; only one in each of September of 1917 and 1918 . It would seem that at least some Victorians had come to believe that Canada did not need the imperial connection to justify its military pride and national self-sufficiency.

---

* *Letters of Travel*, ch. 17, n.p.(www.gutenberg.org/files/12089/12089-h/12089-h.htm)

Throughout all of Canada, of course, the Great War caused massive changes in day-to-day life. The war had been fought on an unprecedented scale. The whole world economy, in fact, had been disrupted as patterns of production and trade were warped. In Victoria, for the first time, local men were part of a mass, citizen army, fighting alongside the "Mother Country" far away in Europe. On the positive side, Britain's need for natural resources, food and manufactured items provided a creative jolt to the local as to the overall Canadian economy. Concurrently, however, the recruitment of Canadian fighting men led to manpower shortages, the growth of trade unions, greater female employment and homes where a father, son or husband lay in a grave in a foreign land.

For several postwar years the *Times*, the *Colonist* and other journals were replete with poetic memorials to these dead youths and men, potential professional and political leaders, unrealized husbands and fathers. Of course, the values and illusions about a glorious war for "freedom" and the "Motherland" did not completely or immediately disappear after the conflict but were accompanied by a profound and understandable grief at the possible waste of so many lives. Shortly before the end of the conflict, a Victoria poet, one **J. Johnson,** expressed a widespread feeling:

Sergt. Henry George Sivertz.
Fell in Battle, September 29, 1918

He would not have us weep,
Although he lies asleep
Amid the fading leaves and flowers of France.
"Each single life is small

When crowns and kingdoms fall",
He wrote before he made his last advance.

And in those tragic fields
Where not a soldier yields,
Conviction's fires outleap the fire of guns;
Where hist'ry of the age
Shall write a crimson page,
Devotion counts him 'mong her splendid ones.

And you, his comrades brave,
Who dug your hero's grave
And laid to rest his youthful form and fair,
You knew his dauntless heart
And how he played his part;
A great man in his youth is buried there.

(*Times* 22 November 1918)
Sivertz, a law student with Thomas R. Robertson, living on Denman Street with his parents, had been killed at the age of twenty-five.

Meanwhile, even before the war began, the conventions of poetry were changing as free verse and a more intellectualized, even obscure, expression found favour in literary circles. Ordinary people, however, continued to write verse and local print media continued to publish it — but on a reduced scale. In more sophisticated verse, scholars have noted the fragmentation of experience and the breakdown of form which reflects the *Zeitgeist* of the postwar years. Writing poetry requires that a person have uninhibited openness to impressions from society or the natural world and the time and place to write. As popular entertainments such as radio, cinema and television absorbed the public's attention, Victoria's newspapers and journals ceased to print verse regularly. The Great Depression of the 'thirties, the Second World War, and the heightened pace of post-war life worked to repress the average educated person's urge to write. Although a city poet laureate has recently been installed in Victoria, social conventions and our "wired world" suggests that never again will British Columbia's capital see the efflorescence of poetry, good, bad or indifferent, that prevailed before 1918.

Today, Victoria is no longer a bastion of imperial Britishness. My own experience may be illustrative. Growing up in the 1940s and '50s, my generation already hated the notion of our home town as "a little bit of Olde England". We had been taught to respect the Empire and the Commonwealth but, travelling abroad in the 'sixties, I discovered that neither meant anything to young Britons. Moreover, my college roommate from Mumbai did not believe that Winston Churchill was a world hero — and for good reasons. Victoria is still a unique city but it can no longer claim to be anything English or even British nor can the "Old Country" still seem to be for Victoria citizens the center of world civilization.

In the twenty-first century, however, at least parts of Victoria are considered "edenic". In 2006 the Community Association of the suburb of Fairfield published *Hanging on to Paradise. An Illustrated Anthology of Community Visions in Prose & Poetry*, suggesting that the association of Victoria with a "Garden of Eden" survives — and expressed in verse!

"The past is a foreign country", said the English novelist L.P. Hartley. And so nineteenth century Victoria may seem to be almost as exotic as that fictional island paradise, "Bali H'ai". Yet they say that travel is broadening. Through it, we become aware of the many varieties of human experience and, by contrast, we come to understand our own culture better. I hope that this tour of Victoria long ago has been "broadening" for my readers.

INDEX